RANDOM HOUSE

Springtime Crosswords

edited by STANLEY NEWMAN

**Random House
Puzzles & Games**

NEW YORK   TORONTO   LONDON   SYDNEY   AUCKLAND

All of the puzzles that appear in this work were originally published in *Newsday*
and distributed nationally by Creators Syndicate.

Please address inquiries about electronic licensing of any products for use on a
network, in software or on CD-ROM to the Subsidiary Rights Department,
Random House Information Group, fax 212-572-6003.

This book is available at special discounts for bulk purchases for sales
promotions or premiums. Special editions, including personalized covers,
excerpts of existing books, and corporate imprints, can be created in large
quantities for special needs. For more information, write to Random House, Inc.,
Special Markets/Premium Sales, 1745 Broadway, MD 6-2, New York, NY 10019
or e-mail specialmarkets@randomhouse.com.

Visit the Random House Puzzles & Games Web site:
www.puzzlesatrandom.com

First Edition

Printed in the United States of America

10 9 8 7 6 5 4 3 2 1

ISBN: 978-0-8129-3626-1

Introduction

Welcome to *Random House Springtime Crosswords,* with 100 warm and breezy puzzles from some of America's most talented puzzlemakers. Each crossword has a theme, or central idea, running through its longest answers. The title provided at the top of each page will give you a hint as to what the theme is. And the answers are all in the back, just in case.

Thanks to Oriana Leckert and Adam Cohen for their help in the preparation of the manuscript.

Your comments on any aspect of this book are most welcome. You can reach me via regular mail or e-mail at the addresses below.

If you're Internet-active, you're invited to my Web site, www.StanXwords.com. It features puzzlemaker profiles, solving hints and other useful info for crossword fans. There's also a free daily crossword and weekly prize contest. Please stop by for a visit.

Best wishes for happy solving!

Stan Newman

Regular mail: P.O. Box 69, Massapequa Park, NY 11762 (Please enclose a self-addressed stamped envelope if you'd like a reply.)

E-mail: StanXwords@aol.com

Join Stan Newman on His Annual Crossword-Theme Cruise!

You'll enjoy a relaxing vacation on a luxurious ship, plus a full program of puzzles, games and instructional sessions. For complete info on Stan's next cruise, please phone Special Event Cruises at 1-800-326-0373, or visit its Web site, www.specialeventcruises.com/crossword.html.

1 EASY COME, EASY GO

by Fred Piscop

ACROSS

1 Director Forman
6 Printer's primary color
10 Healthy look
14 Slack-jawed
15 Seized auto
16 Learning method
17 Hopeless situations
19 Villa d'__
20 Highway overpass support
21 Wiped out
23 Football legend Graham
25 Ticked off
26 Errand runner
30 Team list
33 Nutritive mineral
34 Dress down
36 Awry
39 Longtime UAW head Walter
41 Pertaining to a manuscript
43 Slip into
44 Atelier occupant
46 Actress Heche
47 "Heads up" situation
49 Sweet treat
50 Very, musically
52 Malden or Marx
55 Monogram part
58 Check holders
63 __ of scrimmage
64 Unexpected gain
66 Fireplace filler
67 Wine choice
68 When doubled, a spa site
69 Part of MIT

70 Actor Epps
71 Eat away at

DOWN

1 Microbrewer's need
2 Fictional lab assistant
3 Emit coherent light
4 Makes a choice
5 Military zone
6 Vinegar holder
7 "May I help you?"
8 Did an impression of
9 It smells
10 *Bonanza* star
11 Territory to recover
12 Playful mammal
13 Neglected, as a lot
18 Cockpit abbr.
22 Rubber-tree sap
24 Hockey legend Bobby
26 Encircle
27 Cream-filled cookie
28 Some adoptees
29 Tolkien creature
31 Nag's nosh
32 Proofreader's mark
34 Glacier breakaway
35 Art Deco notable
37 Sharp tooth
38 Go on the lam
40 Asian capital

42 Frat letter
45 Rankle
48 Bear witness
49 On fire, in restaurant lingo
50 Prefix meaning "one thousandth"
51 Vidalia, for one
53 Lum's radio partner
54 Sunburned
56 Bushy do
57 Weaver's tool
59 Leonine sound
60 Opposite of ecto-
61 Exemplar of thinness
62 1/1 song ender
65 Dream Team jersey letters

2 NOTHING MUCH

by Vincent Grasso

ACROSS

1 Acquire
4 Landed, in a way
8 Bar legally
13 Enrich
15 Window filler
16 Expiate
17 Culture medium
18 Early Briton
19 Routines
20 Design pro
22 '61 inauguration poet
23 Ward off
24 Hebrew prophet
26 Wastes time
28 Martini add-ins
32 Outbuildings
35 Sparks and Rorem
37 St. Petersburg's river
38 Leave out
39 Brimless hat
40 Sere
41 Cummerbund
42 Azure
43 Go in __ (put on the dog)
44 Leopard kin: Var.
46 Run away, in a way
48 Put one's __ (intrude)
50 Prepare an egg
53 Partner of alas
56 Paramedic's equipment

59 Japanese-American
60 __ of Judah (Haile Selassie)
61 Language of Pakistan
62 Fallen angel
63 Relaxation
64 Pen pals?
65 Surrounded by
66 Word with dog or bob
67 Gel

DOWN

1 Delighted
2 Like beavers
3 Hint
4 Dismay
5 Café au __
6 Trivial
7 Four: Pref.

8 Hunk of gossip
9 Much ado about nothing
10 In __ (entirely)
11 Change for a five
12 Annoyance
14 Something insignificant
21 Group from Cincinnati
25 Argyles, e.g.
27 Organic compound
29 Extremely
30 62 Across' metier
31 Marquis de __
32 Anjou kin

33 Asian nursemaid
34 Shine's partner
36 Hamilton-Burr encounter
39 Ski lift
43 Difficulty
45 Appropriating
47 Held the first performance
49 Man and Wight
51 Comic Rock
52 Vacillate
53 Anatomical loop
54 Writer O'Flaherty
55 Anent
57 Abie's girl
58 Oxidize

3 BY HOOK OR BY CROOK

by Rich Norris

ACROSS

1 Knocks firmly
5 "__ no idea!"
9 Mundane
14 '60s hairdo
15 Come closer to
16 Collect into a pile
17 Healthful grain part
18 Be concerned
19 Octet plus one
20 "How's that again?"
23 Ames coll.
24 Start of MGM's motto
25 Cohort of Larry and Curly
26 Rhoda's mom
29 Unlawful removal
31 Investor's choice
33 Not up to snuff
34 NRC predecessor
36 Sniggler's quarry
37 Armstrong's music
38 Worry needlessly
42 Meaningless talk, in slang
43 "Balderdash!"
44 Anti-gun-control grp.
45 Tina's ex
46 Small openings
48 Metric weights
52 French sea
53 Liquid in a well
54 Galoot
56 Large container
57 Emote excessively, maybe
61 Go after

63 Algerian port
64 Add to a pot
65 Home entertainment pioneer
66 Subtle quality
67 __ Fiction (1994 film)
68 Central American language
69 Finalized agreement
70 Goes out with

DOWN

1 Bugs, for one
2 From the top
3 Kafka's birthplace
4 Walkman creator
5 Acquire, as debts
6 Big name in publishing
7 Org. for pensioners
8 More soothing, as music
9 Messiah composer
10 Melville novel
11 Missouri port
12 Take advantage of
13 Ft. Collins clock setting
21 Horse opera
22 Apply, in a way
27 Stupefied state
28 Carpenter's tool
30 Meter reading
32 Actress Davis
35 Circle of light
37 Skier's aid

38 Human-powered vehicle
39 Wear out, as a welcome
40 Job responsibility
41 More than suggests
42 Henson or Hutton
46 Dessert container
47 African desert
49 Fifth or Park
50 Runner-up to Maris in '61
51 Drenches
55 Like some codes
58 Scarlett's home
59 Correct
60 Upper limits
61 Symbolic Uncle
62 Greek vowel

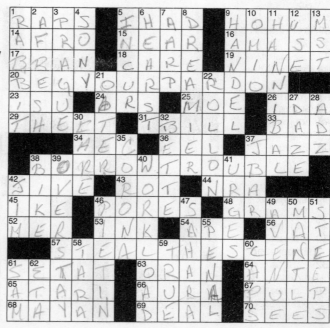

4 IT'S LIKE, DUH!

by Cathy Millhauser

ACROSS

1 Beer need
5 Ditty
9 Golfer gofer
14 Kon-Tiki Museum site
15 Slangy suffix
16 Sit well (with)
17 Prophet suffix
18 "My Heart Will Go On" singer
19 Deviates
20 "Oh, no! Not soft drinks!"
23 Made a deal
24 Turn bad
25 Tom's *You've Got Mail* co-star
28 Bert Bobbsey's sister
30 Blanche's sister
32 Rembrandt wore one
36 City near Turin
39 Frenchman
40 Ling-Ling's inspiration?
43 Han Solo's beloved
44 "Slammin' Sammy"
45 Aconcagua's range
46 Like some check-ups
48 Big roll
50 It's on some Scottish locks
51 A Scottish loch
54 Occupied
59 Lowercase Greek letter?
62 Abner's last name
64 Circular, in product names
65 D-day link
66 Basketball stadium
67 Peas, perhaps
68 Highlander
69 Virtuous
70 Consign to oblivion
71 Largest joint

DOWN

1 Elevate, in a way
2 Richard's *Oklahoma!* collaborator
3 Beach, in Barcelona
4 Without interruption
5 Too-too
6 Writer Murdoch
7 Crying divers
8 Scout rider
9 Frolic
10 Matured
11 Realm of Morpheus
12 German article
13 "You rang?"
21 Agent's cut, perhaps
22 *Calvin and Hobbes* character
26 Give the slip to
27 Opening night dos
29 Fractional prefix
31 Alaska's first governor
32 A neighbor
33 Skater Valova
34 Productive attorney
35 Son of Isaac
37 AL and ME
38 Soften, perhaps
41 Bikini, for one
42 Livy's birthplace
47 Beanie Baby, usually
49 Flowering
52 Fine fiddle
53 Replay technique
55 Audible osculation
56 *Rosmersholm* playwright
57 Julius Caesar was one
58 *La vita nuova* poet
60 *Nox* shiner
61 Hot doll of '96
62 Orange veggie
63 Spanish gold

by Rich Norris

ACROSS

1 Do something about
6 Pulsate
11 Travel on snow
14 Hang loosely
15 ABC executive Arledge
16 Director's cry
17 "Queen of Hearts" singer
19 Poet Emerson's monogram
20 Mid-11th-century date
21 Lincoln's nickname
22 Grin from ear to ear
23 Happen to
25 *Chronicles of Narnia* writer
28 Transgression
29 Raise one's glass
31 __ *Gabler*
33 Golf hazards
34 Gaelic
35 Recovery program, for short
37 Container weight
41 Singer Lopez
43 Balance-sheet item
44 Rush-hour phenomenon
48 IRS employee
49 Like some hair
50 "Again!"
52 Devastate
53 Confess, with "up"
54 About .62 mile: Abbr.
55 Hard to explain

56 Living-room piece
61 Historic time
62 Tax-filing month
63 Velocity
64 German article
65 Cops' routes
66 Fella

DOWN

1 Noun modifier: Abbr.
2 More like a fresh doughnut
3 Rear sections
4 Footnote abbr.
5 Wedding-page word
6 *Jeopardy!* host
7 Sewing-machine inventor
8 Go bad
9 Yoko __
10 Actor Gazzara
11 Threaded fasteners
12 Arabian monarchy
13 List components
18 Zilch, to Zapata
22 Wild animals
24 "__ little teapot . . ."
25 Irene of "Fame" fame
26 Wild guess
27 Cut, as a branch
28 That lady
30 Morality
32 Keep from leaving
35 In widespread use
36 Oklahoma city
38 Imputed

39 Fought off
40 Zeta follower
42 *Mayberry* __
43 HBO rival
44 Walk with effort
45 Oakland athlete
46 Precious stones
47 One of the Brontës
49 Extensive in scope
51 Giraffe relative
53 "Think nothing __!"
56 Truck driver's compartment
57 Reveal, in poems
58 Monk title
59 Tongue-clucking sound
60 Former name of Tokyo

6 WINDOW DRESSING

by Lee Weaver

ACROSS

1 American Uncle
4 Ram's remark
7 Issues an invitation
11 Iowa city
13 Sweet wines
15 __ suey
16 Cantrell or Turner
17 Cowboy's rope
18 O'Hara home
19 Amateur photographers
22 Morning moisture
23 States with force
24 Arm of the Mediterranean
26 Egg-carton amt.
27 Phillie Phanatic, e.g.
29 Dole or Newhart
32 Style of a room
34 Seer's deck
37 Gaucho's gear
39 Pause
41 Greenish blue
42 TV chef Julia
44 Relinquish
46 List-ending abbr.
47 Hullabaloos
49 Cry of discovery
51 Most peculiar
53 Grinds together, as teeth
57 Ungentlemanly sort
58 Performers' acknowledgment
61 Food carrier
63 Prepares eggs
64 Seine tributary
65 Singer __ James
66 Pie-in-the-face sound
67 Fall over one's feet
68 Those over there
69 Chicago Loop trains
70 Fix, as a clock

DOWN

1 Hot sauce
2 Asian nursemaids
3 Computer lists
4 Dutch South Africans
5 Swift horse
6 Aleutian island
7 Part of a play
8 Backyard enhancer
9 Divided nation
10 Salmon do it
12 Filled to the gills
13 Saloon snack
14 Heroic tales
20 Walked heavily
21 Religious offshoot
25 Farm animal
27 Particles of dust
28 Calla-lily family
29 London radio letters
30 Sound of awe
31 First meeting of a sort
33 Relinquish
35 Feedbag morsel
36 RN's specialty
38 Sunburn balm
40 Borge or Cliburn
43 Phonograph record
45 Easier said __ done
48 Ticket ends
50 Wide tie
51 Group of eight
52 Villainous Vader
53 Fancy fetes
54 Splitting __ (quibbling)
55 Borden cow
56 Caught some Z's
59 Something to climb
60 Plow the field
62 Sweet potato

7 FABRICATIONS

by Bob Lubbers

ACROSS

1 Long forward pass
5 Hindu hero
9 "¿__ espanol?"
14 Attention-getter
15 Coup d'__
16 At full bubble
17 Ellington tune
19 Puccini opera
20 High dudgeon
21 Chaplin's wife
22 Certain Japanese-American
23 Lampblack
25 Turkish inn
27 Fruity cooler
28 Delhi wrap
29 Guitarist Montgomery
32 Imp
35 Salk products
36 Plane starter
37 Pig out
39 Aspen A-frames
41 Blend
42 Collars
44 Film on cassette
45 Part of SASE
46 __ Hari
47 Chicken part
48 Self-promoter
50 Papa Hemingway
54 Some transit lines
56 Mrs. Dick Tracy
58 ATM-making co.
59 Surmise
60 Walcott's nickname

62 Mythical weeper
63 Pennsylvania port
64 Billions of years
65 Noses (out)
66 Actress Daly
67 Ex followers

DOWN

1 Fundamental
2 *Butterfield 8* author
3 Parking nuisance
4 ASCAP rival
5 Worked over again
6 "This weighs __!"
7 The blahs
8 Part of A&P
9 Wayne film of 1962
10 "To give her poor dog __"
11 Nast target
12 Dog bane
13 Jai __
18 Noggin
22 Actress Miles
24 Puppeteer Bil
26 Connelly and Antony
30 *The Seasons* painter
31 Mediocre
32 Capitol crown
33 Tied
34 Tormé's nickname, with "The"

35 RBIs, e.g.
36 Adjust
38 Writer Nin
40 Reluctant
43 Pitcher + catcher
46 Dudley and Demi
47 Renter
49 Diving bird
51 Delight in
52 Scottish quick bread
53 Lock of hair
54 Vein site
55 Writer Bagnold
57 The Auld Sod
60 Deep black
61 Archer's bow wood

8 PRIME CUTS

by Patrick Jordan

ACROSS

1. Birthday-party centerpiece
5. Shed a tear
9. Notre Dame's home
14. 23 Across birthstone
15. Confess openly
16. Actress Verdugo
17. Thick mud
18. Tick off
19. Friars Club gala
20. Mayfield moppet
23. World Series mo.
24. Op. __
25. Genetics initials
26. *Face/Off* director
29. Have the goal of
31. Canadian country singer
33. *Strange Interlude* actress
37. Besides
40. Nile snake
41. Doing nothing
42. Youngster
47. More concise
48. Allay one's fears
52. __ roll (doing well)
53. Use the crosshairs
55. Chicken-king connection
56. Ryan or Tilly
57. DiMaggio's nickname, with "The"
61. Slatted shade
63. Assign stars to, perhaps
64. Take a shine to
65. __ Carlo
66. Western author
67. They're mined and refined
68. Hialeah transaction
69. Making __ meet
70. Gets hitched to

DOWN

1. Small jazz bands
2. Individually
3. Discipline learned in dojos
4. Mtn. stat
5. Ajax or Crazy Horse
6. Force out
7. Roper report
8. Suit material
9. Be rife in
10. Facial-tissue additive
11. To the back
12. Personal connections
13. Formed a lap
21. Word form for "outer"
22. Egyptian cross
27. Scott Turow book
28. Tyrannical sort
30. Bowline and sheepshank
32. Hibernation locations
34. More, to Manuel
35. Ember coating
36. Health resort
37. Tenor's neighbor
38. Loan security
39. Going off course
43. Hero's heartthrob
44. Actor Estrada
45. Simi and Silicon
46. Morales of *La Bamba*
49. Strike caller
50. Stunk
51. Way out
54. Enter a highway
55. Behaved
58. Pot contribution
59. Work for
60. Deere device
61. Yuppie auto
62. Mauna __

9 TEMPERATURE'S FALLING

by Lee Weaver

ACROSS

1 Bird beaks
5 Accomplished
8 High-IQ group
13 Bryce Canyon locale
14 MD's org.
15 Reacted to high humidity
16 Author Angelou
17 Letters on a tachometer
18 Nebraska Indians
19 Lose patience
22 Spiritual essences
23 Anglers' needs
24 Onetime TV alien
27 Winter weather concern
30 Tall marsh plants
34 __-bitty
35 Onward partner
36 Ritzy residence
38 Oboist's need
39 Accumulator
41 Overcome unfamiliarity
45 Concorde, e.g.
46 Bay window
47 Central courtyards
52 Food preservation process
54 Showy shrub
57 Miscalculate
58 Lendl of tennis
59 Echo
60 *Apollo 13* director Howard
61 Hawaiian goose
62 Understood
63 __-Cat (Vail vehicle)
64 Matured

DOWN

1 Loses feeling
2 Author Calvino
3 Louisiana inlet
4 Woolen outerwear
5 "Drat!"
6 Put at risk
7 Young ladies to rescue
8 Brunch cocktail
9 Carrier to Ben-Gurion Airport
10 Ultimate degree
11 Mermaid's habitat
12 Computer pop-ups
15 *Who's Afraid of Virginia __?*
20 Felix's roommate
21 Animation unit
24 Fragrant oil
25 Actress Lenya
26 Type of chicken
28 Stashed away
29 Mention for special praise
30 Sidewalk edges
31 Copycats
32 Canary sound
33 Shout of triumph
36 Catchall abbr.
37 Fleece, as a sheep
39 Eccentric sorts
40 Plane-wing part
42 Citizen of Seoul
43 Grab the tab
44 Hurry along
48 Coming out even
49 Inland waterway
50 Nonsensical
51 Nixon running mate
52 Went by quickly
53 James Bond foe
54 Noah's vessel
55 Method of meditation
56 Mil. address

by Norma Steinberg

ACROSS

1 Desire
5 Annoys
9 Syria's president
14 Skin-cream ingredient
15 Forbidden activity
16 Aladdin's buddy
17 Desired result
18 Courtroom offering
19 Singer O'Day
20 New England orchestra
23 Left, at sea
24 Above, poetically
25 Blotch
27 Dashboard abbr.
29 Sailor
32 Motel rooms
33 Grain-storage tower
34 Spoken
35 Robert Young sitcom
38 "You bet!"
39 Evict
40 Rose and Fountain
41 DC title
42 Furniture wood
43 "Golden touch" king
44 Intention
46 Colombian city
47 Spiderlike bug
53 I love: Fr.
54 Deep black, to a poet
55 __ contendere

57 Where Agra is
58 Location
59 Talon
60 Ways and __ Committee
61 Proofreader's marking
62 Verge

DOWN

1 Dogs' tails do it
2 Oodles
3 Biblical shipbuilder
4 Psychic communication
5 Genetic, as a trait
6 Cook a turkey
7 Make a cardigan
8 Recital piece

9 With mouth open
10 Mexican mister
11 Cut with small strokes
12 Small islands
13 Narcs' group: Abbr.
21 Idaho's capital
22 "Uh-uh!"
25 Plumber's tool
26 Giant
27 Capital of Belarus
28 Story line
29 Actress Garbo
30 Garden spots
31 Some sandwiches, for short
32 Crafts for ETs
33 Northern seabird

34 Fido's school subject
36 Spacious
37 __ the beans (blab)
43 Refrigerator decoration
44 __ asst.
45 Brainstorms
46 $100 bill
47 Copenhagen resident
48 Verdi heroine
49 Not so much
50 Newspaper notice
51 Draw for the '49ers
52 Steel-mill refuse
53 Singer Nabors
56 Have debts

WATERY PLACES

ACROSS

1 Fellow
5 Existence
9 Prepare a turkey
14 The Eternal City
15 Arabian sultanate
16 Asia Minor region
17 Les États-__
18 Thoreau's retreat
20 Blanc, et al.
22 Purplish colors
23 Our Miss __
25 Store of provisions
29 Former geopolitical letters
30 Spring holy day
33 Paint layer
34 Of the soft palate
35 Male bee
36 Kellogg's base
39 Cashmere and angora
41 "You __ kidding!"
42 Perry's creator
43 16th-century Venetian painter
45 Actor Stephen
48 Denver team
50 Funny Joan
52 Pavarotti and Domingo
55 1978 co-Nobelist with Begin
56 Fort Bragg neighbor
60 Misplace
61 Switch
62 503, to Caesar
63 Unique sort
64 Multiplied by
65 Ticklish doll
66 Crimsons

DOWN

1 Cookie litter
2 High awards
3 Relative of C major
4 Basil-flavored sauce
5 Despicable
6 Mosque leader
7 FDR's dog
8 Last a long time
9 Trig functions
10 Highly classified
11 Numero __
12 $5 bill
13 Craze
19 Always
21 Trapshooting targets
24 Table staple
26 Chess piece
27 Moving need
28 French summer
31 Maglie or Mineo
32 Grab the tab
34 February greeting card
35 Ranting comic Miller
36 Sugar-cane cutter
37 Dernier __
38 Do parenting
39 Spider's spin
40 Bruins' Bobby
43 Chinese gang
44 Tristan's love
45 Made over
46 Rubbed out
47 Fall flowers
49 Pennies
51 Bravery
53 Exemplar of thinness
54 Milk choice
56 Onetime Atl. crosser
57 __ Beta Kappa
58 Grog ingredient
59 "Old MacDonald" closer

by Rich Norris

ACROSS

1 Masseuse employer
4 Train-schedule listings
9 Female prophet
14 Ice-cream treat
15 Soprano Callas
16 Peddler's merchandise
17 One of Pooh's pals
18 In any way
19 FBI employee
20 "The Raven" poet
23 Advance warning
24 Musical notes
25 Energy
28 Roadside grazer
29 Make a new hole
32 Remain
33 Ere
35 Most healthy
37 *The Song of the Lark* author
39 10 to the 100th power
41 Sky supporter of myth
42 Shakespeare's river
43 Crystal of Hollywood
45 Plant pockets
49 Exaggerate, as expenses
50 Well below standard
51 Greek fabulist
52 *Lonesome Dove* author
57 Red Sea gulf
59 Memorable Hollywood agent
60 Verse opening?
61 Russian Revolution leader
62 Andes beast
63 Commandments count
64 Included afterward
65 Horse fathers
66 A little energy

DOWN

1 Bed covering
2 Frizzy-haired dog
3 Distant orbital point
4 At the head of the class
5 "So long!"
6 Kind of exam
7 Dosage unit
8 Deli selection
9 Exchanges
10 Shakespearean villain
11 More easygoing
12 Kobe currency
13 WWII vessel
21 Charge in court
22 Like news broadcasts
26 Bouncers' requests
27 Dog or cat
29 Auto safety device
30 Baseball stat
31 Window sticker
32 Priest, at times
34 *Alice* spin-off
36 "I get it!"
37 Tree-covered area
38 Braves' home: Abbr.
39 Generation __
40 Eggs
44 Pastoral poems
46 Tough to outwit
47 Where walls meet
48 Looking furtively
50 Label information
51 Distinctive qualities
53 Irish Rose's lover
54 Ivory Coast neighbor
55 Former Russian ruler
56 *Auntie* __
57 In the manner of
58 Abbreviation in a proof

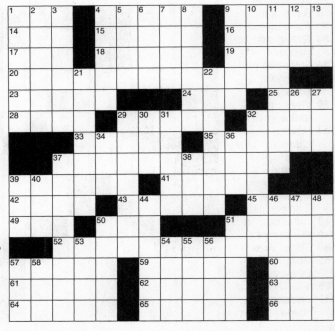

A SWEET GIG

by Fred Piscop

ACROSS

1 Fire starter
6 Howls at the moon
10 Big name in retailing
14 *Exodus* actor
15 Shrinking inland sea
16 Bridge-toll unit
17 Out-and-out
18 Lacoste of tennis
19 Literary figure
20 What a candy inspector did, part 1
23 Jurist Warren
24 "__ had it up to here!"
25 Kingston Trio song
26 Connecticut senator
29 Suffix with rocket or racket
31 Attendance fig.
33 Hoo-ha
34 Make different
36 Reagan confidant
40 What he did, part 2
43 Use translucent paper, perhaps
44 Commonest dice roll
45 Fraternity letters
46 Treater's pickup
48 Queens, to Kasparov
49 *City of Angels* star
50 Vichy, notably
53 Mae West play
55 Bleachers sound

57 What he did, part 3
62 Not fooled by
63 Has __ (is connected)
64 Places to hibernate
66 Singer Redding
67 *The Mod Squad* role
68 Number in black
69 Act the expectant father
70 Kismet
71 Teeny-__

DOWN

1 Dallas sch.
2 Essence
3 Kick in
4 Smelled bad
5 38th-parallel land
6 Quotation source
7 Painter's calculation
8 New Age musician
9 Place for an ace?
10 Tom, Dick, or Harry
11 Self-evident truth
12 Political influence
13 Gossipmonger
21 Breck competitor
22 Sycophant
26 Dotty
27 Polecat's defense
28 Mrs. David Copperfield
30 Shorten again, maybe
32 __ Downing Street

34 The Yanks' div.
35 Awe
37 Author Ferber
38 Complacent
39 Latin being
41 Take measures
42 Forget-__
47 On __ of (for)
49 Fedora feature
50 Dive bomber's descent
51 *Santa Maria* mate
52 Room at the top
54 City near Dayton
56 Attorney-__
58 Car-engine part
59 Fabric fuzz
60 Greet the dawn
61 Small songbird
65 Pig's digs

ACROSS

1 Coarse file
5 Lunar effect
9 Bring to mind
14 Singer Fitzgerald
15 Eur. language
16 Dresser
17 CITY NEAR THE GRAND CANYON
20 Wake-up call?
21 HOSE ENDS
22 "You bet!"
23 Biblical name suffix
24 Ending for million
25 Ward healers?
26 Sphere
27 RR stops
31 Beanpole
34 Hong Kong neighbor
36 Troy sch.
37 COLUMBIA AWARDS THEM
40 __ SUIT
41 Thirsted
42 IRANI METROPOLIS
43 Creative artist
45 Above, to the above
46 Architect Maya __
47 Magician's prop
49 Ready-fire separator
50 Existed
53 "And __ wrote . . ."
55 Benefits seeker
57 CUNARD'S PRIDE
59 *Tiny Alice* playwright

60 Seed covering
61 December song
62 Duffers, once per hole
63 Actor Wilder
64 Classify

DOWN

1 Prepare Mexican beans
2 French street
3 Czechs and Poles
4 Congressional gofer
5 Books, so to speak
6 *The Thrill of __* (1963 film)
7 Auto-__
8 Pixie
9 Box-score item
10 Lightweight weaves
11 Bassoon kin
12 Popular dolls
13 Period
18 EVALUATING
19 TANGANYIKA'S PARTNER
24 Curved
25 Seance sound
26 Mix movie
28 Chi. paper
29 Mimic
30 Agreement in Acapulco
31 Telegram "period"
32 When repeated, a train sound
33 Nerve network

34 Booby-trapped
35 PERFECT
38 ENNOBLE
39 Turned chicken
44 MEDICINE CHEST ITEM
46 Obligated
48 Frank and Murray
49 Actor Delon
50 "Whoopee!"
51 MORE LIKE THE MARXES
52 Chamberlain epithet
53 Bulrush
54 Greek goddess
55 Wax finish
56 Peaks: Abbr.
57 Arabian tea
58 Fall behind

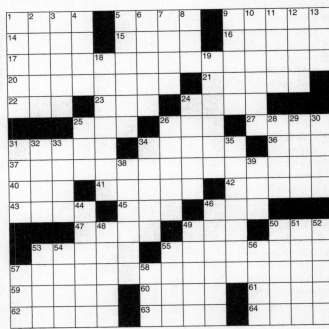

15 OUTERWEAR

by Rich Norris

ACROSS

1 Takes illegally
5 Bar mitzvah presider
10 Tra-__
14 Colorful fish
15 Lightweight synthetic
16 Trojan War hero
17 Painter's application
19 Perplexing path
20 Neutral vowel sound
21 Director Preminger
22 Born and __
23 Ballpark official
25 Gumshoe
27 South African peninsula
35 Asian arena, for short
36 College official
37 Yankee manager
38 The Bard of __
40 Dress designations
42 Water carrier
43 Prepares potatoes, in a way
45 Inheritance factor
46 Plaything
47 Like espionage operations
51 Free (of)
52 Knight's title
53 Read quickly
56 Southwestern stewpot
60 Not tight
64 Mata __
65 Hardcover's covering
67 Peepers
68 *Dallas* matriarch
69 Guitarist Clapton
70 Forest growth
71 Reporter's angle
72 Impetuous

DOWN

1 Singer Diana
2 Oil grp. since 1960
3 One of music's "Three B's"
4 Make an appearance
5 Divining tool
6 With the bow, in music
7 Ink smudge
8 Dock docker
9 Completely
10 Shari Lewis puppet
11 Slightly open
12 Lounge (around)
13 Chopped down
18 Identify
24 Pea holders
26 Summer hours in MD
27 Be picayune
28 Mobil competitor
29 Represent falsely
30 Looked (at)
31 Continuously
32 Speak pompously
33 Earlier in time
34 Hard to hang on to
35 Antidrug officer
39 Close call
41 Adriatic and Aegean
44 Hit the slopes
48 Sun-dried bricks
49 __ monster (lizard)
50 Food-store owner
53 Son of Noah
54 Boxing win
55 Angers
57 Lie (about)
58 *Damn Yankees* vamp
59 Related by blood
61 Gumbo ingredient
62 Spanish half-dozen
63 Engrave deeply
66 Airport arrival

16 STADIUM CLUB

by Fred Piscop

ACROSS

1 Theater sections
6 Wrestling surface
9 Out of whack
14 Don't exist
15 Goof up
16 Corday's victim
17 One less than hexa-
18 Stephen of *The Crying Game*
19 River to the Missouri
20 Clinton's milieu
23 Cartoon Chihuahua
24 Unceasingly
25 Blue ox of legend
28 Menagerie units
31 On the briny
35 Author LeShan
36 Buddy, Max, or Bugs
37 Weasel kin
38 Salinger character
42 Fiery crime
43 Blotch
44 Born, in the society pages
45 Actress Patricia
46 Washbowl
48 Edible ears
49 Chapters of history
51 Transcript fig.
53 Business hub
60 Theater of old
61 VCR button
62 Hardy, to Stan
63 Influence
64 In the past
65 Serenity
66 Circus setups
67 Nol of Cambodia
68 Barber's sharpener

DOWN

1 Reindeer herder
2 Hydrox rival
3 Lee or Grant: Abbr.
4 In one piece
5 One of fifty
6 Popular car make, for short
7 Neck of the woods
8 "The Rose of __"
9 Love, Italian-style
10 Flashy Italian auto
11 Home to some Kurds
12 Long story
13 __-Foy, Quebec
21 Ancient Peruvian
22 NY's Park and Madison
25 Irish playwright Brendan
26 Be crazy about
27 Glider wood
29 Truman's nuclear agcy.
30 Astroturf alternative
32 Dictator's helper
33 Conger catcher
34 Eve who played Miss Brooks
36 One of an ice-cream duo
37 Repeatedly, in rhyme
39 Gave sparingly
40 News org. created in 1958
41 *"Ars __, vita brevis"*
46 __-relief
47 Stellar
48 Medicinal shape
50 Pipsqueaks
52 Falls rudely
53 Just hanging around
54 Illuminating gas
55 __ Park, Queens
56 Clickable symbol
57 Controversial apple spray
58 Role for Edward G.
59 Don't give up
60 Autumnal mo.

17 TEACHER'S PESTS

by Patrick Jordan

ACROSS

1 Singer Fitzgerald
5 Prospector's property
10 Humorous poet
14 Laugh heartily
15 Ben on *Bonanza*
16 City near Santa Barbara
17 Classroom taboo
19 Box-office total
20 Keats composition
21 Side squared, for a square
22 Joan's *Dynasty* role
24 Archaeological sites
25 Order on an octagon
26 Prayer beads
29 Filled with pithy passages
33 Authorizes
34 Kin of "Heck!"
35 Serb or Pole, e.g.
36 Suburban sale venue
37 Works hard
38 *Compos mentis*
39 On __ with (equal to)
40 May weekend race, for short
41 Shrivel
42 Family histories
44 Vern's bumbling buddy
45 Tennis titan Arthur
46 Shipboard slammer
47 Expeditious
50 Like a drumhead
51 "Friend or __?"
54 Clothier Strauss
55 Classroom taboo
58 Accessible to everyone
59 Taxpayer's terror
60 Designer Cassini
61 Actress Anna May
62 __ down (berate)
63 The former Miss Truehart

DOWN

1 Consequently
2 Garish, as some garments
3 Like some excuses
4 Circle segment
5 Ordained group
6 Chad and Rob
7 Melody at the Met
8 Quaint lodging
9 Explosive units
10 Classroom taboo
11 Comet rival
12 H.H. Munro's pen name
13 Makes haste
18 Goosebumps raise them
23 Parking place
24 Classroom taboo
25 Ill-tempered
26 Kingly
27 Giraffelike creature
28 Wrapping plastic
29 Chewed portions
30 Burn brightly
31 Highway divisions
32 Momentous occasion
34 Charity recipient
37 Penny pincher
41 Compose prose
43 African snake
44 Emulates Etna
46 Underlying principle
47 Field furrower
48 __ *Man* ('84 Estevez comedy)
49 Bakery appliance
50 It may be stemmed or turned
51 Manicurist's tool
52 Small bills
53 Coop clutches
56 *Ben-__*
57 Deteriorate

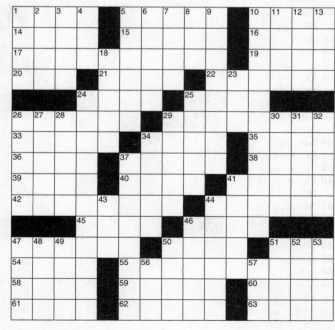

FRAT PARTY

by Randolph Ross

ACROSS

1 Egypt's Port __
5 Role for Shirley
9 Flying pest
13 Cadet's coll.
14 __ Pascal (programming language)
16 Downhill racer
17 Had too much souvlaki?
19 They may have it
20 __ cell (erythrocyte)
21 Go with
23 Bee participant
24 *My Name Is __ Lev*
25 Slalom track shape
26 Pear-shaped instrument
27 Josh
30 Scams
33 __ Dame
34 Walk outside Mir
35 Louis, e.g.
36 Aegean transportation?
38 Call a game
39 Turkish VIP
40 Links targets
41 "Hey, you!"
42 Fraction of an inch
43 Ballpark figs.
44 Elevator cage
46 Wane
48 Memorable Henry Fonda role
52 Confound
54 *The Seven-Per-Cent __*
55 Public scenes
56 Show relief in Rhodes?
58 Yield
59 Muscle contraction
60 Tiny sound
61 Till filler
62 Memo abbr.
63 Epochs

DOWN

1 Plaintiffs
2 __ in the right direction
3 Manilow's "__ It Through the Rain"
4 Engages occasionally (in)
5 "And so __" (Ellerbee catchphrase)
6 Grapevine item
7 Wilbur's horse
8 Litigator's org.
9 Cold dessert
10 Some Greek-Americans?
11 Maturing agent
12 Audition
15 Fat substitute
18 Woes
22 Ream unit
24 Road fillers
26 Brain sections
28 Singer Burl
29 Nutty
30 Small amount
31 Oft-quoted catcher
32 Greek dessert?
33 *Lorenzo's Oil* actor
36 Big birds
37 Inexpensive lodgings
41 Record for future airing
44 Op-Ed piece
45 Be adjacent to
47 City vehicles
48 Perch
49 More mature
50 Where sailors go
51 Little pieces
52 Bit in a salad
53 First place
54 ASAP, in the ER
57 Ecol. watchdog

19 SENSE OF DIRECTION

by Lee Weaver

ACROSS

1 Autobahn vehicle
5 Made a basket
9 Sgt.'s subordinate
12 Fishline hangup
13 Pots and kettles
15 Start of a quip
17 Pitch __-hitter
18 Cat's prey
19 Inc., in London
20 Fiber from a cocoon
22 Quip, part 2
28 Rajah's land
30 Old-style knife
31 March Madness org.
32 Bird berths
33 Jelly-filled pastry
35 Blasting caps?
36 Quip, part 3
40 Testing place
43 Winglike
44 Metropolitan
48 Memo notation
50 Filled with reverence
52 Moon valley
53 Quip, part 4
56 Western lily
57 Signal an actor
58 Trim a tree
60 Sunday talk topic
61 End of quip
66 Hardly tasty
67 Ogler
68 Dancer Charisse
69 Surreptitious sound
70 Cincinnati sluggers

DOWN

1 Silly
2 Opens a map
3 Doris or Dennis
4 *Young Frankenstein* role
5 Lateral measurements
6 Spanish gold
7 German surname starter
8 Med. specialist
9 Swiss state
10 Labor result
11 Author Wallace
14 Like *Time*: Abbr.
16 Union in Detroit, initially
17 B-ball connection
21 Acquaintances
23 Came on stage
24 Audition (for)
25 Spooky
26 Bled, as colors
27 Have a snack
29 On the ocean
34 Guided trip
37 Jai __
38 First light
39 *Exodus* author
40 Community ordinance
41 "__ see it . . ."
42 Theater level
45 Holy
46 African capital
47 Las Vegas illumination
49 Like an egret
51 Sweet-sounding
54 Tidy the garden
55 Mystery-story pioneer
59 Jury member
61 "Attack, dog!"
62 Apple seed
63 Pts. of tons
64 Capp and Capone
65 Soapmaker's need

20 REPEATERS

by Vincent Grasso

ACROSS

1 Loses elasticity
5 Actress Turner
9 Discussion group
14 Fictional frightener
15 French islands
16 Author Jong
17 "__ I say, not . . ."
18 Evening illumination
20 Richly decorated
22 Muddy the waters
23 Soil turner
24 *It's a __ . . . World*
25 Checkout units
27 Blood component
29 Withdraw
33 Colorado clock setting: Abbr.
35 Pea place
37 Glass shard
38 Tony or Emmy
41 Name, as a knight
43 Silt deposit
44 Wild ones
46 "La-di-__!"
48 Start for wit or picker
49 Minstrel-show figure
50 Valentine blooms
53 Put on a pedestal
56 Native American drum

59 That woman
62 Parka pullover part
63 Parka part
64 Mélange
67 Dastardly
68 Mumbai land
69 Earth's crust layer
70 Actress Russo
71 *For __ My Gal*
72 Midterm, e.g.
73 Snick-or-__

DOWN

1 Genesis city
2 Greek meeting place
3 Stadium seating area
4 "Open __!"
5 In a row
6 MacGraw or Baba
7 Pola of silents
8 Like __ (swiftly)
9 Headlong
10 Onassis, for short
11 Almost, in poems
12 Sound reflection
13 Not on time
19 Layers
21 Road goo
26 Word form for "shadow"
28 *The __ Squad*
30 All tied up
31 He loved Lucy
32 Prefix for while
33 Labyrinth
34 Stately bird
36 Failure

39 Ottava __ (Italian verse form)
40 Free-ticket recipient
42 Local tavern
45 Nosy one
47 Unenviable position
51 The sun
52 Arab rulers
54 Pigeon perch
55 Fisher or Foy
57 Like a ewe
58 Free-for-all
59 Tapered metal piece
60 Ready the razor
61 Icelandic poetry
65 Card-game cry
66 Baseball execs.

21 POOL TIME

by Lee Weaver

ACROSS

1 Mideast missile
5 Barbecue materials
10 Rouse from sleep
14 Singer Guthrie
15 Radiant
16 "__ it!" ("Aha!")
17 Prefix meaning 46 Across
18 Reinforce
19 Isolated
20 Riverboat propeller
23 Loser at Gettysburg
24 Member of the clergy
28 '50s Ford
31 Nickname for General Arnold
34 *Gone With the Wind* star
35 NFL team
36 Certain warplane
38 Swelled head
39 Hazard a guess
40 Psyche parts
41 Area under a house
44 *Bus Stop* playwright
45 Aquarium fish
46 Small digit
47 Snit fit
48 Flavorful seed
50 Model Carol
51 Decorated procession piece
57 Stinging insect
60 German submarine
61 Asta's owner
63 Girlfriend, in Grenoble
64 Regular writing
65 Son of Seth
66 McNally's partner
67 Circus worker
68 Collector's quests

DOWN

1 Golfer Snead
2 Farm output
3 Forearm bone
4 Scribbles
5 TV signal carrier
6 Folklore villain
7 "There ought to be __!"
8 Scottish body of water
9 Wield a broom
10 Winner of 1066
11 In the past
12 Writer Kesey
13 Summer, in Lyon
21 Dover's state: Abbr.
22 Therefore
25 Subsiding
26 Heavy hammer
27 Less long-winded
28 Expels
29 College accomplishment
30 Summer ermines
31 Zoo heavyweight
32 Birdlike
33 Coventry coins
36 Scale starts
37 Spelling contest
42 Prepared a present
43 Buddhist monk
44 Chants
47 Everybody
49 Spew forth
50 In search of
52 Incantation opener
53 Adverse fate
54 Smooth the way
55 Top-of-the-line
56 Horse's gait
57 Armed conflict
58 Physicians' org.
59 Go astray
62 Donkey

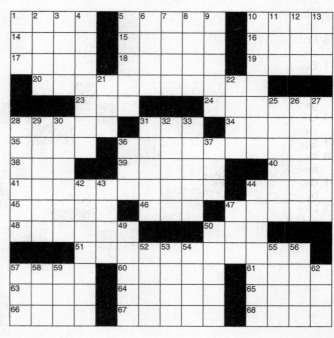

ACROSS

1 Saucy
5 Knights' armor pieces
11 Derisive snort
14 Director Kazan
15 Flowering shrub
16 *I __ Camera*
17 Stingy
19 '60s platters
20 Vexation
21 W. __ Maugham
23 Poet's Muse
26 Scam
27 River through Berne
28 Academic meeting
30 Flyers
32 __ Paulo, Brazil
33 Rhythmic flow
36 Prone to shoplifting
41 Everyday business
42 Old card game
44 Li'l Abner creator
47 Eire
50 It's bought by the bar
51 Grp. once led by Arafat
53 Like some jackets
54 Go on a tour
57 __ carte
58 *Printemps* follower
59 Clumsy
64 Three times, to a druggist
65 Admiration
66 Dynamic start
67 Grad. class
68 Palestinian ascetic
69 Father

DOWN

1 Hound or hamster
2 Whitney or Wallach
3 Equip a ship
4 Gauguin's retreat
5 Nightspot
6 Israeli gun
7 Lariat
8 Singer John
9 Abound
10 *Vic and __* (old radio show)
11 Christmas fir
12 French physicist
13 Hie
18 Sci-fi film of 1982
22 More uncommon
23 Half a figure eight
24 Genuine
25 Mine: Fr.
26 Dexterity
29 Throw a tantrum
30 Ruffle one's feathers
31 Ade cooler
34 Early 6th-century date
35 Film composer Morricone
37 Chart
38 School dance
39 Panache
40 Wrapped up
43 Unusual
44 Resources
45 Hang out
46 Basketball players
48 Queen of scat
49 Woody vines
51 Fuel materials
52 Dike
55 *Of __ I Sing*
56 Cong. meeting
57 "Alas!"
60 Yearning
61 "*Agnus __*"
62 Transgress
63 John or Jane

23 FEMINIST LITERATURE

by Rich Norris

ACROSS

1 Facts, briefly
5 Slippery-textured fabric
10 Guernsey, e.g.
14 Heath-covered tract
15 Utah city
16 Reason for a handshake
17 With *The*, James novel
20 State since 1890
21 Wipes away
22 Wily
23 "For shame!"
26 Pup's peep
27 Bale contents
30 "__ Rebel" ('62 song)
32 Tee follower
34 Steakhouse offering
36 Glare reaction
39 Functions
40 With *The*, Odets play
42 Modern Persian
44 Showing faith
45 Split down the middle
47 Table support
48 Bounce back
52 Word in many Commandments
53 Okla. neighbor
55 Help
57 Chop off
58 Met productions
61 Midway alternative
63 With *An*, Hellman autobiography
67 Diplomacy breakdown
68 Flora's partner
69 Brownish purple
70 Humorist Ogden
71 __ and blood
72 Zipped along

DOWN

1 Full of mischief
2 Bit of pasta
3 Surprise attacks
4 "Straight" word form
5 Mineral spring
6 *Exodus* character
7 Carry
8 Tusk material
9 "That's cheating!"
10 Not active
11 Beachcomber's find
12 Little shaver
13 Bridge expert Culbertson
18 Go bad
19 Anti-inflammatory drug
24 Avoid
25 Actor Carradine
28 Word of agreement
29 Word of agreement
31 In agreement
33 Sign up
35 Pianistic raconteur
37 Accelerate
38 Competitive and intense
40 Rejects
41 "Thank Heaven for Little Girls" musical
42 Son of, in Arabic names
43 River, in Spain
46 Import fee
49 Refuse to talk
50 Newsman Greeley
51 Let in the first customer
54 Like Fran Drescher's voice
56 Jones' partner
59 Essence
60 Andrew of *Melrose Place*
62 Brewing ingredient
63 Ode subject
64 Talk-show host Peeples
65 Nav. rank
66 Morse bit

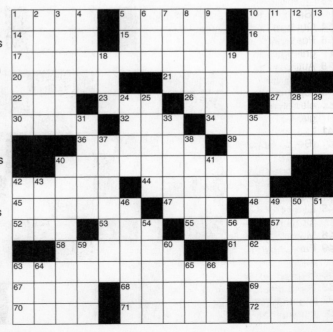

FROM JEERS TO CHEERS

by Cathy Millhauser

ACROSS

1 With 2 Down, the *Enterprise* saga
5 Domino, e.g.
9 Tyne's family
14 *Alfred* composer
15 Piedmont province
16 Magazine installment
17 Is born a patsy?
20 Lacking details
21 Ear problem
22 Wrath
23 Narnia lion
25 Oniony rappin'?
29 Neck-bent assent
32 Former Milan moolah
33 __ *et Lui* (Sand novel)
34 Queeg's craft
36 Post-grad grilling
38 Author Wallace
39 Henry's son
40 Japanese electronics giant
41 "__ Around" (Beach Boys song)
43 Unhearing
44 British record label
45 Like some furniture?
48 Madrid museum
49 Fund-raising abbr.
50 Ritzy appetizer
53 Imagine
57 Auto mechanic's innovations?
60 Similarly
61 Eye layer
62 Custer associate
63 Some TVs
64 Big knell
65 Former speeders from JFK

DOWN

1 Needs a lift?
2 See 1 Across
3 Start to date?
4 With unease
5 Bush-whacking knife
6 Wan
7 Actor Gilliam
8 Kipling work
9 Light-year, e.g.
10 John who married a Duke
11 Exam for an atty.-to-be
12 Cosmonaut Gagarin
13 Places (on)
18 Israeli port
19 __ sci (coll. course)
23 Fast movement
24 Pierce, perhaps
25 Miserly
26 Grant's real first name
27 Rial spender
28 United, as nations
29 Japanese-American
30 Hoopster Shaq
31 Earthenware from Holland
35 Certain thigh muscles
37 Teacher of Plato
42 Representative
46 Actor Rhodes
47 *Art of the Fugue* composer
48 Hard to please
50 Apr. midnight-oil burners
51 Woodstock name
52 Self-inflating?
53 Appeal of courts
54 Four-stringed instruments
55 '96 Tony-winning musical
56 Placido's "those"
58 Trophy, often
59 "Hi, Claudius"

by Norma Steinberg

ACROSS

1 Military fliers: Abbr.
5 Room dividers
10 Untidiness
14 Baguette or croissant
15 Prufrock's creator
16 Actor Montand
17 Defense org.
18 Gray or Hamilton
19 Steakhouse specification
20 100 pence
23 Oxidize
24 Slack
25 French sculptor
28 Hippie's money
31 Primates
32 Washes thoroughly
34 Energy
37 Explore new boundaries
40 "Poor baby!"
41 Robust
42 Concept
43 In a __ (quickly)
44 Boob tube
45 King or Arkin
47 French cheese
49 Save for the future
55 Swindle
56 "There was __ woman . . ."
57 "When __ a lad . . ."
59 Run in neutral

60 No longer fresh
61 City on the Tiber
62 Outdo
63 Bart's father
64 *Born Free* lioness

DOWN

1 Vase
2 *General Hospital*, e.g.
3 Sax range
4 Prosper
5 Fuses metal
6 Most desired invitees
7 Pocket residue
8 Ore vein
9 Constellation component

10 Innumerable
11 Actor Maurice
12 Sturdy fabric
13 Compass reading
21 Religious figure
22 Charter
25 Entranced
26 Artistic work
27 Office furniture
28 Wallace or Noah
29 Talk wildly
30 A deadly sin
32 Culinary artiste
33 Page in a book
34 Pea holders
35 Fencing sword

36 __ moss
38 Cogitate
39 Party animal
43 Part of a suit
44 Pablo's aunt
45 Stage whisper
46 Hangs around
47 "__ of the Ball"
48 Actress Winona
50 Squash
51 Not fooled by
52 Linguist Chomsky
53 Missing GI: Abbr.
54 Thanksgiving tubers
55 Overalls part
58 Ocean

26 MEAL PEOPLE

by Bob Anderson

ACROSS

1 New Zealand bird
5 "Get lost!"
9 Land or sea ending
14 __ instant (quickly)
15 "Quiet!"
16 Of Antarctica, e.g.
17 Comic actor's courses
20 Locomotive power
21 What X marks
22 Shopper's sheet
23 Tattoo word
25 Columnist Bombeck
27 Arthur of tennis
30 The Trojans
33 Auto inflatable
37 Explorer Heyerdahl
38 Puts one's foot down, hard
40 Narcissist's problem
41 Singer's side dish
44 Metallic rock
45 Start of a play
46 "Uh-uh!"
47 Mermaid movie
49 Pompous one
50 One with debts
51 Rug variety
53 __ Tomé and Principe
55 Singer Kristofferson
58 Red ink, symbolically

61 Beatle with the sticks
65 Justice's java
68 Really go for
69 Carson's predecessor
70 Coffee vessels
71 Like mesh
72 Excitable
73 Ill-gotten gains

DOWN

1 Smooch
2 Monogram unit: Abbr.
3 Walk in water
4 Privately, to a lawyer
5 That boat
6 Swear
7 PDQ
8 Pang
9 Reducing salon
10 Shirt part
11 Jai __
12 Steno's books
13 Prefix for while
18 I love: Latin
19 Like some gowns
24 Radio City, for one
26 __-en-scene (stage setting)
27 Element's IDs
28 Like a tack
29 Vacation housing
31 Proofreader's "leave it"
32 Winter warmer
34 Downstairs, shipwise
35 With jaw dropped

36 Champion of the theater
39 Belgian town
42 Lid attachment
43 Sot's quantity
48 Categorize
52 Get crazy
54 Remark from Chan
55 Genghis or Kublai
56 Not at all polite
57 "__ Rhythm"
59 Abundance
60 Malden TV series of '80
62 Spheroid hairdo
63 Casino town
64 Take it easy
66 Turkish governor
67 Johnnie Ray song

27 TO SOME DEGREE

by Rich Norris

ACROSS

1 Cooking fat
5 Next year's jr.
9 Syrup source
14 Part of the eye
15 Patella's place
16 Garfield's middle name
17 Bridge calls
18 Tabloid fodder
19 Lions and Tigers
20 Best man's job
23 Airport listing, for short
24 Sick-day cause
25 With good judgment
28 Turn back
30 Take it easy
33 Deer's mom
34 Fall behind
36 Debussy's "La __"
37 Put in a hold
38 Home feature
42 Gardener's need
43 Collarless shirt
44 Insignificant amount
45 Biblical vessel
46 Bit of debris
48 Prepares for a fight
52 Two-speaker system
54 Blockhead
56 Tommy follower?
57 Pasternak novel
61 In progress
63 Smog consequence
64 First victim
65 Conductor Walter
66 Land in the ocean
67 Entangle
68 Buffet patron
69 Tourney type
70 Quarterback's call

DOWN

1 Inexperienced sailor
2 Emulate Lindbergh
3 Railroad employee
4 Short race
5 Competence
6 Traveling, as a rock band
7 Look searchingly
8 Rope fiber source
9 Mathematical array
10 Helps a hooligan
11 Asked for intervention from
12 Get away
13 Printer's measures
21 Key of Beethoven's Emperor Concerto
22 Oscar and Edgar
26 Weaving apparatus
27 Bow tree
29 Choice word
31 Fireplace remnant
32 Shelter
35 Become commercially successful
37 *Duck __* (Marx Brothers film)
38 Satirist Sahl
39 Invited to the movies, maybe
40 Actor Stephen
41 Martini's partner
42 Suffers from
46 Pie-chart piece
47 Impress deeply
49 Asian peninsula
50 "The King of the Cowboys"
51 Shoulder scarves
53 TV executive Arledge
55 Brightness
58 State on Lake Erie
59 Carpentry tool
60 Jazz accompaniment
61 '60s Justice Fortas
62 Monk's moniker

28 VEGGIE PLATE

by Fred Piscop

ACROSS

1 Scrub, NASA-style
6 FedEx rival
9 Most of Iberia
14 Conical abode
15 Tuck's partner
16 Broom ___ (comics witch)
17 Main part
20 Join the navy
21 Pitcher's stat
22 "*Mangia!*"
23 Have to have
25 New currency in the Old World
28 Popeye's success formula, in his own words
34 Suffix for tank
35 Center X
36 Political refugee
37 Trick-or-treaters' wear
40 Task
42 Scarecrow stuffing
43 A third of a half-inning
45 "She loves me ___"
47 Slalom curve
48 Attackers in a 1978 cult film
52 Together, musically
53 Dueler with Hamilton
54 Playwright Shepard
57 Bench-press unit
59 Japan foe of 1904-05
63 Is proficient
67 Chip giant
68 Attendance fig.
69 Makes bootees
70 Apt to sulk
71 Judge Bean
72 Ancient lawgiver

DOWN

1 "Don't throw bouquets ___ . . ."
2 "___ there, done that"
3 Milky gem
4 Eye spot
5 Wonderland dishes
6 Sturm ___ Drang
7 Snowman accessory
8 Mushroom cells
9 ___ Na Na
10 Orchestra's workplace
11 Sunburn soother
12 Creative input
13 Tweed's caricaturist
18 Underground experiment, briefly
19 Brownish gray
24 Key relative to B min.
26 Tire holders
27 "Put a lid ___!"
28 Farsi speaker
29 Detroit debacle
30 "Money-saving," in product names
31 Match up
32 Totally unrefined
33 Chops down
34 In a frenzy
38 Tropical nut
39 Took to court
41 Zero-star movie
44 Cape Cod town
46 Bull word form
49 Adolescent
50 Pool wear
51 *Twelfth Night* duke
54 Milk choice
55 Part of AD
56 Marquand sleuth
58 Cancún cash
60 Potter's need
61 Division word
62 Org.
64 Take the plunge
65 Full of guile
66 Porker's pad

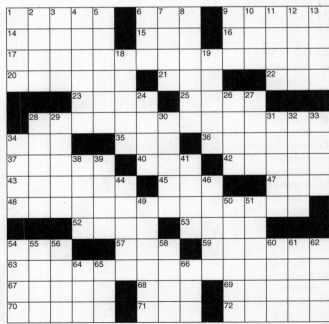

29 HOMING IN

by Richard Silvestri

ACROSS

1 Make a video
5 *Atlantic City* director
10 Talisman
14 In good shape
15 *A Lesson From __*
16 Mill material
17 Homer's favorite kind of golf?
19 Boot block
20 Give-go filler
21 Put down, on the street
22 Jupiter spacecraft
24 Is unable to
26 Sacred song
27 Lose ground?
29 Make possible
33 Trojan War hero
36 Commanded
38 Sci-fi character
39 Punch ingredient?
40 Out of whack
42 Masculine principle
43 Stand
45 __-cake
46 Native of 5 Down
47 Vacation spot
49 "Hernando's Hideaway," e.g.
51 Guest work
53 Ill-fated
57 McIntosh kin
60 __-mo
61 "Bravo!"
62 Knight's neighbor
63 Homer's heraldic display?
66 Non-pro
67 At attention
68 Journey
69 Gain prerequisite
70 Bumper bumps
71 Rocky pinnacles

DOWN

1 Something to talk about
2 Japanese woofer
3 Idolater
4 Check out
5 Prairie province
6 Backdrop for Heidi
7 Reed of rock
8 Dismiss
9 What you will
10 Homer's power grab?
11 Kind of vaccine
12 Slugger Canseco
13 Aware of
18 Taste stimulus
23 Advance
25 Homer's closest relative?
26 Assist with the negotiations
28 Reduce the vibration of
30 Sty male
31 Subway system component
32 Upper hand
33 Way out there
34 Agree
35 Sale stipulation
37 Are, in Aragón
41 Diamond settings
44 "__ Tu" (1974 song)
48 Roughed out
50 Blunder
52 Fungus starter
54 Cuban castle
55 Glue eponym
56 Newspaper posts
57 End of a shooting
58 New York college
59 Reply to the Little Red Hen
60 Dunkers or Shakers
64 Gymnastic perfection
65 ABA member

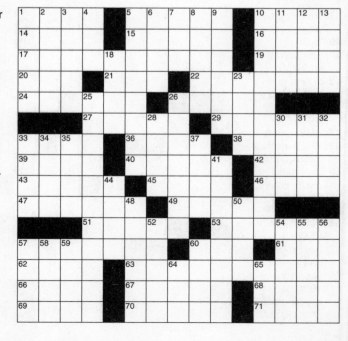

NOT SO HOT

by Lee Weaver

ACROSS

1 Ship's pole
5 Baby's word
9 Sharpen
13 Florence's river
14 Musical melodrama
16 Angelic light
17 Simba, e.g.
18 Scots and Welsh
19 Persia, today
20 Croquet spots
22 Publisher's unsolicited manuscripts
24 Fill to the brim
26 General vicinities
27 Determining capacity
30 Canadian capital
33 Deprives of confidence
35 Does the dog paddle
37 Inc., in London
38 Long (for)
41 Zilch
42 Legal claims
45 Harding's successor
48 Put in a pleat
51 Elate
52 Pokes
54 On a cruise
55 In a precarious situation
59 Mr. Fudd
62 Garden implement
63 Author Calvino
65 Bullets, for short
66 State solemnly

67 Yo-Yo Ma's instrument
68 *Nautilus* captain
69 Not as much
70 Profound
71 Wee serving

DOWN

1 Teen's hangout
2 14 Across highlight
3 Overwhelms with work
4 Merchant ship's capacity
5 One of Snow White's pals
6 *Planet of the __*
7 TV angel Reese

8 Maestro Toscanini
9 Two-person cutting tool
10 Mata __
11 Airline to Israel
12 Muscle quality
15 Valuable quality
21 Recipe direction
23 Beanies and berets
25 Green-eyed monster
27 Aquatic bird
28 Playful prank
29 "That's amazing!"
31 Large sailing ship
32 Buddy, in Barcelona
34 Cul de __
36 Weaver's reed

39 Milne marsupial
40 Bright star
43 Sibling's sons
44 Delhi dress
46 __ majesty (high crime)
47 The Emerald Isle
49 __ boom
50 Fixed a manuscript
53 Actor's minimum wage
55 College exam
56 Church section
57 Boxing wins
58 *Vogue* competitor
60 Jane Austen novel
61 House component
64 "Alley __!"

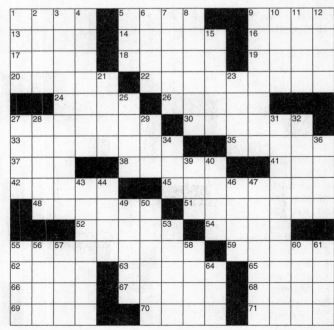

31 SEEING RED

by Rich Norris

ACROSS

1 Brazilian dance
6 Heat source
11 Cool dude
14 Same old same old
15 Kind of lily
16 Vein pursuit
17 Clue character
19 Cal. page
20 Frat letter
21 Resistance unit
22 Rhythmic feet
24 Winter flower
29 Routing need
30 Lifted
31 Part of BLT
34 *The Age of Reason* author
35 Call __ day (retire)
38 Musical composition
39 Computer command
40 School grps.
41 __ canto
42 Without company
43 Try to corner the market on
44 Accuse falsely
46 Anthem preposition
47 Chekhov play, with *The*
51 *Lou Grant* character
52 Hill climber
53 Fast flier
56 Gardner of *On the Beach*
57 Alabama eleven
62 NYSE regulator
63 War hero Murphy
64 Ancient region of Asia Minor
65 Stat for McGwire: Abbr.
66 Gets closer to
67 Smallville family

DOWN

1 __ pump (drainage aid)
2 Warts and all
3 Orchestra offering
4 __-relief
5 Unsuccessful one
6 Hoaxes
7 Road covering
8 Plumbing connection
9 Tap choice
10 Painter Henri
11 Article of trade
12 Mideast residents
13 Short and sweet
18 Poker ante, often
23 "__ we having fun yet?"
25 Med. plans
26 Sports team employee
27 Battleship to remember
28 "__ That a Shame"
31 Hope of Hollywood
32 Big galoot
33 Blind alleys
34 TV spot
36 Kind of cross
37 Cobra
39 Dramatic presentation
40 Contented sound
42 __ violet
43 '50s hipster
45 Hosp. sections
46 "That's terrible!"
47 Enter uninvited
48 Hang in midair
49 Docket items
50 Islamic spirit
54 Get to work on *Time*
55 Afternoon socials
58 Wish one hadn't
59 Actress Lupino
60 Russian space station
61 Sock front

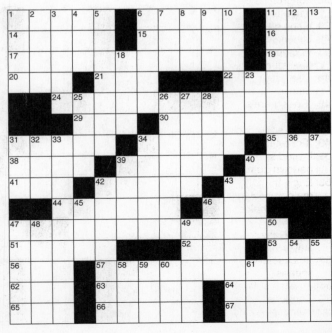

ACROSS

1 Goes downhill
6 __ Alamos, NM
9 Duelers' distances
14 Lofty roost
15 Appropriate
16 Dieter's temptation
17 Half a city name
18 Pullman, e.g.
19 Watercourse
20 One of Charlie's Angels
23 Diddly
24 Suffix for planet
25 Childish
27 x and y, in equations
32 Sloth's home
33 One __ customer
34 Not as nasty
36 Long-distance haulers
39 Goes off course
41 Low point
43 Recipe guesstimate
44 Composer Saint-__
46 "Sour grapes" writer
48 Corp.'s top dog
49 "Forget it!"
51 Invited to perform again
53 English mathematician
56 Make a choice
57 Totally
58 Eliot Ness player
64 Stockholm sedans
66 __-pitch softball
67 Condor's clutcher
68 Host a roast
69 Pipe bend
70 In the know
71 Al of *Today*
72 Formerly named
73 Street show

DOWN

1 Trims two-by-fours
2 Jacob's first wife
3 __ Stanley Gardner
4 *Gunsmoke* marshal
5 Critter with flippers
6 Like a doily
7 Moonfish
8 Standee's support
9 Vince Lombardi's eleven
10 Altar constellation
11 Baseball's "Grand Old Man"
12 Cyberspace letters
13 Room, in Rouen
21 Newsman Newman
22 Director's "Stop!"
26 Epitome of thinness
27 Western Indians
28 Author Ephron
29 *Nashville* actress
30 Final Four grp.
31 Meal with matzoh
35 Respond to reveille
37 "So that's it!"
38 Sporting sandals
40 Hoity-toity type
42 Futuristic servant
45 Not so dense
47 MTV favorite
50 Often-inflated item
52 NHL city
53 More contemptible
54 Santa Anna target
55 Clampett portrayer
59 Model Macpherson
60 Spade, to Bogart
61 Winged
62 Reactor site
63 Patch place, perhaps
65 Wax producer

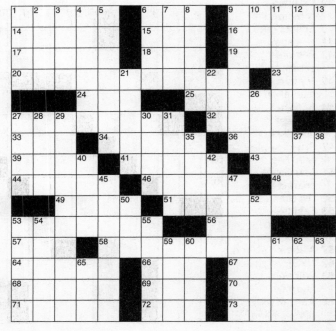

33 CARRY A TUNE

by Bob Lubbers

ACROSS

1 Enticement
5 Probability
9 Part of HUD
14 Foot span
15 Superman's mother
16 Alan Ladd classic
17 West Indies instrument
19 Sudden increase
20 Attacking
22 TV talker
23 City subways
26 Cops' quarries
28 One of HOMES
29 Goblin starter
32 Israeli carrier
33 Magnani and May Wong
35 *Aida* composer
37 River of China
40 Profundity
41 Epoch
42 Pun reaction
44 Retirees' fund org.
45 General Doubleday
47 Time of day: Fr.
48 *Camelot* actor
50 Asian holiday
52 Nasty ruler
53 Norman Rockwell quality
56 "__ we the lucky ones!"
58 Joyce of *Roc*
59 Samba relative
62 Centric starter
64 Jazz style
68 Concerning
69 2001 follower
70 Yugoslav marshal
71 Vaudevillian Nora
72 Helper: Abbr.
73 Ginger __

DOWN

1 Coll. degrees
2 High-school course
3 Bar rocks
4 Epithet for Alexander
5 Not really new
6 Fix, in a way
7 Medication
8 Philippine island
9 Nav. designation
10 Cuban dance
11 Jazz style
12 Ire
13 Necessities
18 Card game
21 Two-__ sloth
23 Honey beverages
24 Sea eagles
25 The pop-tune world
27 *Bounty* captain
30 Rotisserie, e.g.
31 Special Forces cap
34 Puppeteer Lewis
36 Uncommon
38 Clear plastic
39 Motionless
43 Takes back
46 Autumn pear
49 May or Stritch
51 Small-time
53 Recovery program
54 "Maria __" (Dorsey song)
55 Molten rock
57 Old French coin
60 Pirate quaffs
61 "How sweet __!"
63 Where grads are lts.
65 Family
66 Greek letter
67 Blouse, e.g.

34 TWO CENTS' WORTH

by Patrick Jordan

ACROSS

1 Plumbing problem
5 Half of the "Monday, Monday" group
10 Trojan War hero
14 Harass
15 Embarrass
16 Have the moxie
17 "Calling" company
18 Frutti forerunner
19 Marker fillers
20 Minimal money
23 Actress Harper
24 Dutch cheeses
28 Catches sight of
31 Camera type: Abbr.
32 Expert fighter pilot
33 Minimal money
36 Sprint rival
37 Allows to
38 Two-kind link
39 Dumbo's wings
40 __ Baba
41 Minimal money
45 __ Got a Secret
46 Yonder damsel
47 Sam and Alistair
48 It had a part in the Bible
50 The King and I setting
51 Minimal money
57 Play the lead
60 Wreck

61 1994 Jodie Foster film
62 Midwest Indian
63 Send spirits soaring
64 Makes mad
65 Depend (upon)
66 Broad valleys
67 Top rating

DOWN

1 Study all night
2 Not prerecorded
3 Awful aroma
4 Science of heredity
5 The Piano Lesson painter
6 Shares a border with
7 James' Gunsmoke role
8 Hammett hound

9 Roofing tile
10 "Farewell, François!"
11 Comic actress Hooks
12 Genesis boat
13 __ out (deletes)
21 Cheat at hide-and-seek
22 Parachutist's pull
25 Lustrous fabric
26 Increase gradually
27 San Andreas fault phenomena
28 Rich pastry
29 Do a librarian's task
30 Felt sorry for
31 Naval commando

34 Film genre
35 Very loudly, on a score
39 Narcissist's affliction
41 Kojak, to pals
42 Showed a response
43 Eave danglers
44 12 Down builder
49 Flower arrangement
50 Condition
52 African tree
53 Kin of etc.
54 Rex Stout detective Wolfe
55 Crooner Campbell
56 In addition
57 Knightly title
58 Baby's "piggie"
59 Beltmaker's tool

35 HEADY STUFF

by Lee Weaver

ACROSS

1 Singer Judd
6 Rib order
10 Civil-rights activist Parks
14 Frequently
15 Spicy stew
16 __ out a living (barely got by)
17 Blends batter
18 October birthstone
19 Entreated
20 Amaze
23 Presidential nickname
24 Junior, for one
25 Give one's avid attention
31 Furry fish eater
35 Very seldom
36 "__ o'clock scholar"
38 Unrefined metal
39 On a cruise
40 __ Park, CO
42 Diva's solo
43 Wistful wishing
44 Scottish hillside
45 Became strained
47 List of candidates
49 Exactly
51 Part of TGIF
53 Always, in poems
54 Very appetizing
61 Sky bear
62 Dismounted
63 British peers
66 High schooler, usually

67 Days of old
68 Barker's pitch
69 Rocky peaks
70 Person bringing a case
71 Dance for two

DOWN

1 Turndown words
2 To the rear, on a boat
3 Elevator maker
4 Nothing more than
5 Put into place
6 Andy of *60 Minutes*
7 Purina brand
8 Highlands family
9 Curly cabbages

10 Feel contrite
11 Tex. neighbor
12 Fortuneteller
13 Says more
21 One who heeds
22 Before long
25 Donkey sounds
26 Studio stand
27 Sports complex
28 Meadow
29 Gobbled up
30 French holy woman: Abbr.
32 Human trunk
33 Iroquoian Indians
34 *The Cloister and the Hearth* author
37 Old Testament book

41 __ Paulo, Brazil
42 Raggedy doll
44 Sibling of Jo, Meg, and Amy
46 Most spooky
48 Powerful ones
50 Move unsteadily
52 Weaves back and forth
54 Mongrel
55 Sandwich cookie
56 Consumer
57 Baseball manager Felipe
58 Car component
59 California wine valley
60 Smile ear-to-ear
64 Table part
65 Highway warning sign

36 BRACE YOURSELF

by Rich Norris

ACROSS

1 Grade-school basics
5 Hit the mall
9 March honoree, for short
14 Martial-arts stratum
15 Relate
16 Welsh canine
17 "I cannot tell __"
18 Neighborhood
19 Assortments
20 Helping hands
23 I, to Claudius
24 Pince-__ glasses
25 Says
28 Prom, e.g.
30 Portable coolers
32 Compete
33 Subsiding
36 Bird house
37 Spreadsheet number
39 Score higher than
41 Strengthened, as muscles
42 Paintings and such
43 Gear elements
44 Like seven Nolan Ryan games
48 Bahamas capital
50 French friend
52 "Born in the __"
53 Mail destination
57 Manual skill

59 Facts and figures
60 Mid-12th-century date
61 Sadat of Egypt
62 Kids' school: Abbr.
63 Cobbled together
64 Low-voiced one
65 Hindu garment
66 Chimps and baboons

DOWN

1 Reduced in rank
2 Caviar source
3 Like some bow ties
4 Baby-book first

5 Astonished look
6 Avis rival
7 Bullfight shouts
8 Take the field
9 Highlands clan
10 Available, as an apartment
11 Age-old
12 Gone by
13 "__ the season . . ."
21 Ryan or Tatum
22 Ra, for one
26 Trucker's truck
27 Go out with
29 Coagulate
30 Helsinki residents
31 First chip
34 Extinguish, as a fire

35 Urban blight
36 Guitar device
37 Scam victims
38 Caesarian attire
39 Legal deterrent
40 Important time
43 Caribbean leader
45 Wheel cover
46 Arthurian lady
47 Prepares to take off
49 Couches
50 Subsequent to
51 Home of the Heat
54 Pindar products
55 Presidential pooch
56 Poet Lazarus
57 Urban vehicle
58 Genetic initials

37 JOYRIDING

by Bob Frank

ACROSS

1 Seaweed
5 Winter warmer
10 Pitch indicator
14 City of Spain
15 Of an arm bone
16 Portent
17 !
18 Simpleton
19 Desire
20 Leisure-time vehicle
22 Seat weaver
23 Whopper
24 Steadfastness
26 Reference book
30 ___ la la
31 Actor Marvin
32 Leisure-time vehicle
38 "Last of the Red Hot ___" (Sophie Tucker)
41 Rosin holder
42 Take ___ (try)
43 Leisure-time vehicle
46 Actress Gardner
47 Assist
48 Lets off
51 Perplex
56 Crux of some riddles
57 Take to the soapbox
58 Leisure-time vehicle
63 1958 film musical
64 Ruhr Valley city
65 Kingly address
66 College subj.
67 Plateaus
68 Vitality
69 Yin partner
70 Ski trail
71 Pats

DOWN

1 Priestly garments
2 Frog step
3 Auction ender
4 Actress Lansbury
5 Ray of light
6 History Muse
7 Moffo and Magnani
8 Sped in the direction of
9 Young fish
10 Lately
11 Muscat native
12 Credo
13 Spreadsheet jotting
21 Cacophony
22 About
25 Env. contents
26 Charity
27 Not fatty
28 Office message
29 The Virginian actor
33 Skater Babilonia
34 Make eyes at
35 Cartoonist Addams
36 All-conquering thing
37 Zeta followers
39 In the wings
40 Show pleasure
44 Like most prime numbers
45 Outlay
49 Wrigley Field player
50 Still wrapped
51 One over par
52 1999 Emmy role
53 Kid's wheels
54 Ford collectible
55 Outbreak star
59 Lowest high tide
60 Arizona river
61 Clutch
62 Desires
64 Printer's measures

ACROSS

1 Bogs
5 Bridge call
9 Picture transfer
14 Oratorio piece
15 Leave out
16 Gladden
17 Noted trailblazer
19 Neck scruffs
20 Averred
21 "__ a million years!"
23 Can. province
26 __ *With Wolves*
29 Some brooks
33 Everlasting, old-style
34 Came up
35 Pie favorite
37 Tony-winner Hagen
38 "Mona __"
39 Paragon
40 Peeved mood
41 Cure hide
42 Put up
43 "__ *bleu!*"
44 Shoe padding
46 Mockingbird cousin
48 City on the Delaware
49 Government center
50 Slogan writers
52 Lightly colored
57 Blackjack call
59 Old radio show

62 Deep blue sea
63 Fogy
64 Fashioned
65 Snooty retort
66 "Verily!"
67 Epochal segments

DOWN

1 Crazes
2 Part of QED
3 Hirschfeld's daughter
4 Table condiment
5 Toy dog
6 Latin 101 word
7 Impiety
8 British carbine
9 Toothed, as leaves

10 Galahad's mother
11 Kids' cereal
12 Devoured
13 Guitarist Paul
18 Memphis street
22 *Island of the Blue Dolphins* author
24 Swap
25 Visual appearances
27 Full
28 Usher, e.g.
29 Like Latvia
30 Richards of *Jurassic Park*
31 Ships' petty officers
32 Eagle org.

36 Newsreel name
39 Papas or Dunne
40 Stockholm airline
42 Component
43 "__ Doll"
45 Third on a match
47 Turns in, in a way
51 Nothing, in Nicaragua
53 Appellation
54 Growl
55 Icelandic poem collection
56 Batik colors
57 On a roll
58 Here: Fr.
60 May honoree
61 "__ to Billie Joe"

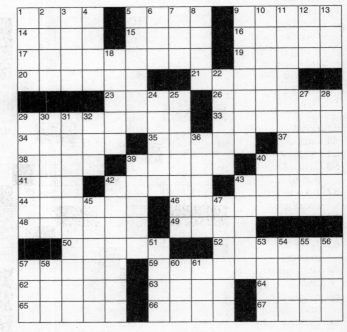

39 SWEET AND NUTTY

ACROSS

1 It's sweet and nutty
9 Makes new plans
15 Estrange
16 With malice
17 VIPs
18 Very long term
19 Kirk's diary
20 Half a screen twosome
22 French summers
24 Striper, for short
25 Force down
27 Hebrew letter
28 Gods' group
29 Harem rooms
30 '84 Olympics no-show
32 Cartoonist Hoff
34 UFO pilots
35 Reduce
38 Garment part
40 Conk
41 Erhard's program
44 Barrie baddie
46 Rate
48 Expedition
50 Discordia's counterpart
54 Get high
55 Russian cooperative
56 Talk like crazy?
57 *Mission: Impossible* actor
60 Nevertheless
61 Place apart

62 Goldwyn discovery
64 Shepherd
65 Health program
66 Photographic systems
67 They're sweet and nutty

DOWN

1 Moms of comedy
2 Onetime mayor of San Francisco
3 Set up
4 School of meditation
5 ___ uproar
6 Anderson et al.
7 Workshop
8 Fed's family
9 Space-shot segment
10 Greek reveler's utterance
11 Have a ___ (intend)
12 Surveyor's devices
13 Sandbox associate
14 Roget wd.
21 Alsace affirmatives
23 Secure
26 Clandestine signal
31 "What did I tell you!"
33 Engraved stamp
35 *Sesame Street* lesson

36 Deli stock
37 One with hives
39 ___-do-well
42 They make us feel embarrassed
43 South Seas staple
44 Less lenient
45 McGraw of *The Commish*
47 Extremely fast
49 Tread heavily: Scot.
51 Wickerwork
52 Belong
53 Rockin' rollers?
58 Gunk
59 Ship out
61 Capable?
63 Part of MS

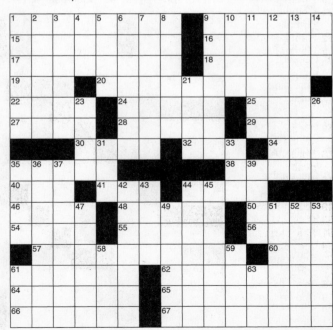

40 DANCE FEVER

by William A. Hendricks

ACROSS

1 Moves like a rabbit
5 Bird call
10 Singer Wooley
14 *Grapes of Wrath* character
15 Taylor of *The Nanny*
16 Answering machine cue
17 Australian tune
20 CBS symbol
21 Dueling sword
22 "___ Your Love Tonight" (Elvis song)
23 Cornfield menace
24 Flower part
26 System
29 Nuts and ___
30 Realty unit
31 Columbus' birthplace
32 Ram's remark
35 Candy bars
39 Keystone Studios character
40 Light blues
41 Jai ___
42 "Bess, ___ My Woman Now"
43 Burger King rival
45 *Bon ___!*
48 Frog relative
49 Works hard
50 Puts on
51 Pas' partners
54 Joey Dee & the Starlighters song
58 To ___ (perfectly)
59 Showed on TV
60 Sore
61 Sly Foxx

62 Safecracker's "soup"
63 Squarish cereal

DOWN

1 Hockey great Gordie
2 Approve
3 Rock heap
4 Ready to go
5 Camera stand
6 Extend a contract
7 *Bus Stop* playwright
8 Moon lander
9 Grassy area
10 Tours of duty
11 ___ putt (finish on the green)
12 Bitter-___ (diehard)
13 Like some eyes

18 Goose egg
19 Ovoid mint
23 *Mask* star
24 They're unacceptable
25 North Carolina college
26 "___ the Knife"
27 Sonic bounce
28 Golf hazard
29 Alphas' followers
31 Astronaut's wear
32 Blend
33 On vacation
34 Flea-market tag
36 Chinese philosopher
37 Prefix for lateral
38 Round of applause
42 Squealed

43 Is not acceptable
44 National League division
45 Face-valued
46 French versifier
47 ___ up (spoke)
48 Copy-machine supply
50 Incriminating info
51 It's west of Wis.
52 Arthur of tennis
53 Underworld river
55 Showed on TV
56 1002, to Caesar
57 WWII lady in uniform

ACROSS

1 Character actor Eric
6 __ kebab
11 Play segment
14 Flax fabric
15 NBC morning show
16 __ Paulo, Brazil
17 *Pretty Poison* star
19 Paid athlete
20 Coarse file
21 Story
22 Adherent: Suff.
23 Very long time
25 Plain speaking
27 Forest element
28 Alaskan bay
30 Slather on
32 Mr. Pulver's rank
33 Simple sugars
35 Endure
36 Jack Webb's *Dragnet* role
39 Leave alone, to a proofer
41 Arabian Sea gulf
42 Colt morsel
45 Strain
47 Navigators' instruments
49 Social equal
50 German merchant guild
53 Singer Jerry
54 Coach Parseghian
55 Woody's son
56 Actress Drescher
58 Balderdash
59 Early evangelist
63 Ascot
64 Lloyd Webber musical
65 Mall unit
66 Append
67 Update a clock
68 Color gradations

DOWN

1 Deli order
2 Brooklyn campus: Abbr.
3 Burdensome
4 Treat icy roads again
5 Finishes
6 Pig digs
7 Bookstore section
8 Brainstorms
9 French rooms
10 Jekyll's counterpart
11 Strives for, with "to"
12 Infant's auto accommodation
13 Honked
18 Put in proximity
23 Imitate
24 Flying fisher
26 Sloop hazard
27 Waiter's load
29 Caterwauls
31 Factory
34 Sp. woman
36 Scoff
37 Altar exchanges
38 Some coffees
39 Cortisone, e.g.
40 Paid the tab
42 Interminably
43 Part of A&P
44 Mao __-tung
45 Ancient Greek city
46 Confess to a priest
48 "Let's go," in Livorno
51 ". . . calm, __ bright"
52 Actor Nick
55 But: Ger.
57 Corrode
60 Sun __-sen
61 Garfunkel or Carney
62 Affirmative answer

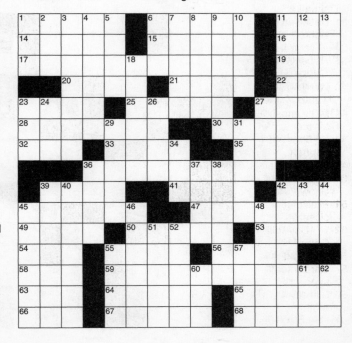

LUMBERJACKING

by Rich Norris

ACROSS

1 Heat source
4 Heat source
9 Radioer on the road
13 Prefix with gram or graph
14 __ Rica
15 Topic
16 Political favor-monger
18 Intended (to)
19 Trapper's trap
20 *Airwolf* actor
22 Like some tomatoes
23 Sun. follower
24 Become mature
25 Antediluvian
26 Wally Cleaver portrayer
28 Depressing situation
31 Unskilled worker
33 All together
36 *Rebel Without a Cause* actress
40 Whirling waters
41 MGM mascot, for one
44 Be about to happen
47 RN's specialty
50 Enjoy Mount Snow
51 Prefix for classical
52 "__ Day Will Come"
55 Draw out
57 Carpenter's support
60 Biblical brother
61 Humorist Nash
62 Frequent Yo-Yo Ma collaborator
65 Villainous looks
66 State-fair attractions
67 Be in the red
68 Gets it wrong
69 Keep for later use
70 Great, slangily

DOWN

1 Become solid
2 Peter or Paul
3 Agreed to terms, formally
4 Made a point
5 City of Spain
6 Immigrant's subj.
7 Mr. T's TV outfit
8 Thomas of *That Girl*
9 Stylishly elegant
10 Lament
11 Come out
12 More flushed
15 April payment
17 Like the seafood in sushi
21 Provide funds for
22 Absorb, with "up"
27 Sag in the sun
29 Oklahoma native
30 Sheep product
32 Church area
34 Never, in Nuremberg
35 High schooler's book
37 Heavy weight
38 Zeal
39 Become faded
42 Island off Japan
43 Annual basketball tourney
44 Shoe part
45 Barely adequate
46 After-bath application
48 Near-ringer
49 Contract provision
53 Employers
54 Word on an invoice
56 Choler
58 Towel word
59 Switch positions
63 Ruckus
64 Signed, in a way

43 ASSUME THE POSITION

by Fred Piscop

ACROSS

1 Dreadlocked one, for short
6 Butter servings
10 Duffer's headache
14 Sweater synthetic
15 Cut and paste
16 Verdi heroine
17 Olmos film of '87
20 Toward the rear
21 Orpheus' instrument
22 Actor Wallach
23 Singer Della
25 City on the Loire
27 Telly network
30 Band booster
31 Fine-tune
32 Verdi piece
34 Letter after theta
36 Weasel out of
40 Take five
43 Use finger paint
44 MacDonald's partner
45 Lacking couth
46 Connections
48 Always, poetically
50 More: Sp.
51 Solidarity name
54 Polar drudges
56 *Exodus* character
57 British streetcar
59 "All the world's __"
63 Shirk one's responsibilities
66 Toy-block brand
67 Division word
68 How some popcorn is popped
69 Overwhelmed with humor
70 Theater ending
71 __ Alegre, Brazil

DOWN

1 Sub __ (secretly)
2 Crafts' partner
3 Shutter strip
4 Copier additive
5 __ *Doria*
6 Cross product
7 Discombobulate
8 Shipshape
9 Caterer's fuel
10 Mai __
11 Fastener for Rosie
12 Fred's dancing sister
13 Left Bank city
18 Lacking vitality
19 Score in horseshoes
24 Hub-rim connectors
26 "When pigs fly!"
27 Stream striper
28 Porkpie feature
29 Give a ticket to
31 *Messiah* composer
33 Die down
35 Son of Abe
37 Styptic stuff
38 Ernst's style
39 Partners no more
41 Noble Brit, briefly
42 Textile-plant container
47 Nocturnal insect
49 Send again
51 Squash-court features
52 Historian Durant
53 Feudal lord
54 Chew the scenery
55 Dictator's assistant
58 __ Domini
60 Not shut tight
61 __ alone (solo)
62 River through Aragón
64 Mathers costar
65 Neither's partner

44 P.O. BOXES

by A.J. Santora

ACROSS

1 Confine
6 Psyched
10 Director Reitman
14 "Goodnight" girl
15 The moon
16 Do a takeoff on
17 Italian city
18 Jingoistic god
19 Bump into
20 Mills Brothers song
23 Thurman of *Pulp Fiction*
24 Stag, e.g.
25 Verb tense
30 Volga Basin people
34 Big Internet provider
35 Mexican appetizer
37 Adjoin
38 Go to extremes
42 Brunei's home
43 Chops up
44 Itty-bitty
45 Breastbones
48 Made over
50 The skinny
52 Jose's aunt
53 Approving unquestioningly
60 Exploding star
61 Alliance since 1949
62 Showery month
63 Fourth person
64 Grad
65 Arizona city
66 Ring
67 Vic's radio wife
68 Clear

DOWN

1 Butterbean
2 Lily kin
3 Card combination
4 Stuck
5 Catfish Row dwelling
6 *Sustineo __* (USAF motto)
7 Expert
8 Upright
9 Joint sealer
10 Like Olympians
11 Look at
12 Communicant's word
13 Becker barrier
21 Andrew's ex
22 Teachers' org.
25 Grandfatherly ones
26 Get out of bed
27 Cow girl?
28 On the rocks
29 __ *Finest Hour*
31 "Life Is Just __ of Cherries"
32 Pakistani money
33 1998 role for Fiennes
36 Formerly
39 Game for some businesspeople
40 Third-largest asteroid
41 Figure
46 Pen point
47 Punta __, Chile
49 Motormouth
51 Song sounds
53 Bench outfit
54 Eye part
55 Card game
56 Big book
57 __ *La Douce*
58 Pinches
59 Mirth
60 Rug texture

45 FUELISH TALK

by Lee Weaver

ACROSS

1 Fighter's punches
5 Moby Dick seeker
9 Son of Seth
13 Singer Fitzgerald
14 Weighing device
15 Bathe
16 Forest songbird
18 Saber cousin
19 Letter insert: Abbr.
20 Film holder
21 Movie awards
23 Renter
25 Water-balloon sound
27 Sharp flavor
29 Idolizing
33 Helped with the dishes
36 Hard to find
38 Sudden thought
39 Water: Sp.
40 Caesar's tongue
41 Applaud
42 Something to fill out
43 Urban thoroughfares: Abbr.
44 Hangs on to
45 Sawhorse, e.g.
47 Patriot Nathan
49 Word of welcome
51 Swelled
55 Good-tasting
58 Show team spirit
60 Dockworker's org.
61 Ukrainian city
62 Car with low fuel efficiency
65 Singer Adams
66 To the left side, on a ship
67 Boundary
68 Water source
69 No longer here
70 Thumbs-down votes

DOWN

1 Emerald or ruby
2 Unaccompanied
3 Voting groups
4 Down in the dumps
5 Ranch unit
6 Pulls with force
7 Gore's namesakes
8 Obligated
9 Shocking fish
10 California wine valley
11 Exceeding
12 Understands
14 Glossiness
17 Tire feature
22 __ Paulo, Brazil
24 Digging machine
26 County, in Louisiana
28 Sand/pebbles mixture
30 Not doing much
31 Tide type
32 Mountain passes
33 Float on the wind
34 Frankenstein's assistant
35 Untainted
37 Had a hot dog
40 Loaf around
44 Clumsy person
46 Three times, in a prescription
48 More or less
50 Welles of filmdom
52 Actress Radner
53 Melancholy poem
54 Offers a challenge
55 Deviate
56 White House staffer
57 Bride's headgear
59 Folklore monster
63 Mil. address
64 Method of meditation

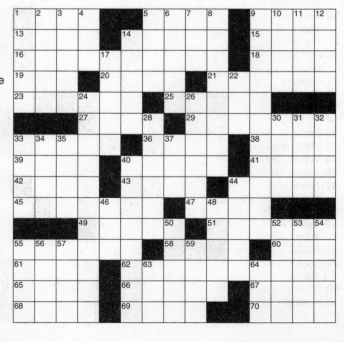

ACROSS

1 Run playfully
5 Location
9 Diarist Nin
14 ". . . __ saw Elba"
15 Detective's quest
16 Least beneficial
17 Hayloft site
18 Milliner's wares
19 In check
20 Doubter's statement
23 Distinctive manners
24 Looked searchingly
28 Gloss target
29 Retrieve
31 "Slithy" thing, to Carroll
32 English county
35 Former immigration island
37 Hair application
38 Consider carefully
41 __ polloi
42 Boca __, FL
43 Helps a hood
44 Wallet stuffers
46 Machine part
47 NBA great Erving's nickname
48 Type of angel
50 Roman orator
53 Repetitive bore
57 Layered rock
60 Eagerly excited
61 Draped garment
62 Completes a road
63 London art gallery
64 List ender
65 Pile up
66 Shelley works
67 Unit of force

DOWN

1 First name in country music
2 Postgraduate hurdles
3 Commendable quality
4 '50s kids' show host
5 Carry
6 Broadway offerings
7 Inning enders
8 Analyze
9 Cognizant
10 Soon, perhaps
11 Bet-hedging trader, for short
12 "This __ stickup!"
13 Unkempt place
21 Alchemist's preparation
22 Kind of nerve
25 Scoundrel
26 Happening
27 Shoulder muscles, briefly
29 __ and doom
30 Ardor
32 Community spirit
33 River to the Rhône
34 Aspen visitor
35 Feminine ending
36 In short supply
39 Salsa dipper
40 Was opposed (to)
45 Dark brown furs
47 Sad songs
49 Fourth estate
50 Twenty fins
51 Tough to dig in, as soil
52 Church instrument
54 Green Hornet's assistant
55 "My word!"
56 Broad valley
57 Fitness center
58 Smoked meat
59 Actress Gardner

GOOD VIBRATIONS

by Paula Zimmerman

ACROSS

1 Soft leather shoes, for short
5 Rock guitarist Clapton
9 WWII sub
14 Longfellow bell town
15 Jacob's wife
16 Soda flavor
17 Malt-shop orders
20 Very successful
21 Art __
22 *Swiss Family Robinson* author
23 Former Cremona cash
25 *Birth of a Nation* group
27 Manage somehow
30 Struck down
31 Sailor's milieu
34 Sailors' school: Abbr.
35 The Charles' terrier
37 Author Joyce Carol
39 Pirate's exclamation
42 Lugs along
43 Small bills
44 Suffix meaning "vision"
45 "All right!"
46 Benefit
48 Still in the box
50 Fanne once in the news
51 Barracuda variety
52 Pitts of the movies
55 Alternatively
57 Blazing
61 Political troublemaker
64 Siouan tribesmen
65 Urban eyesore
66 Big shot
67 Lawncare need
68 Slow flow
69 Diving-bell inventor

DOWN

1 Some computers
2 Roman emperor
3 Reptilian menace
4 Union member's benefit
5 House extension
6 British novelist
7 "I can't believe __ the whole thing!"
8 Last word in chess
9 Word of disgust
10 Muscles
11 Like some trees
12 Zoo attractions
13 Kinski role
18 Egg-shaped
19 Arias
24 Outcry
26 Physicist's study
27 Damp-smelling
28 ". . . who lived in __"
29 Makes mittens
30 *Gypsy* composer
31 Phases
32 Unexplainable
33 Syrian leader
36 Like some ashtrays
38 Reversal
40 Standard Oil of New Jersey, once
41 "The jig __!"
47 Cut down
49 Nifty
50 Signal flare
51 Musical bridge
52 Rise sharply
53 Flivver
54 Put (away)
56 Bargain time
58 Chichen __ (Mayan city)
59 Highway
60 Acts human
62 Neighbor of Leb.
63 Little devil

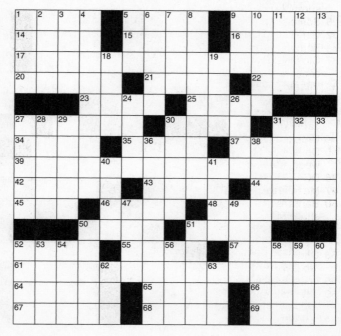

48 CENTER FIELDERS

by Fred Piscop

ACROSS

1 Roll-call vote
4 Beach playthings
9 Dopey, e.g.
14 Cassowary cousin
15 Palmer, to his followers
16 *Star Trek* lieutenant
17 Respond to an SOS
18 "With parsley," on some menus
19 *Midnight Cowboy* role
20 Try to knock out, maybe
23 Grand __ National Park
24 Tram filler
25 Legalese surname
28 Some skirts
32 Ulna's neighbor
34 Pompous sort
37 Clothing buyer's concerns
39 Vittles
40 Landmark Mickey Mouse cartoon
44 Urges to attack
45 Do some woolgathering
46 DC VIP
47 Mesmerized
50 Barber's sharpener
52 Shirt with a slogan
53 Churchill's "so few"
55 Local theaters
59 Title for Prince Andrew
64 "Later!"

66 __ Gras
67 Sawbuck fraction
68 *Joie de __*
69 Maze word
70 No-win situation?
71 Ten-percenter
72 *The Boys of Summer* shortstop
73 __ up (angry)

DOWN

1 Bread ingredient
2 Rousseau book
3 Taxpayer's dread
4 Irreligious life
5 Saroyan's *My Name Is __*
6 Letters at Calvary
7 Caddy competitor
8 Omega competitor
9 Pioneer automaker
10 "Huh?"
11 Accesses a stored phone number
12 Santa Fe and others: Abbr.
13 __ Schwarz
21 Lap dog, for short
22 Blow it
26 Navel variety
27 Ruhr Valley city
29 Penpoint
30 Shirt with a reptilian logo
31 Burns slightly
33 Costa __ Sol

34 Number in black
35 Popular kiddie-lit author
36 Frank's opposite
38 Scratch a dele
41 Flat __ pancake
42 Realm of Ares
43 Springsteen tune
48 Like car-radio buttons
49 Wee bit
51 Pony up
54 Ticked-off one
56 Vendor's area
57 Bert's buddy
58 Airborne targets
60 Phone, slangily
61 Welles role
62 Art Deco notable
63 Poems of praise
64 An ex of Frank
65 Archeological site

49 ANCIENT ODOMETRY

by Patrick Jordan

ACROSS

1 Diminish
6 Abandon, in a way
10 Afternoon socials
14 NASCAR competitor
15 Freshly
16 Invective
17 Start of a quip
20 Tined table tool
21 Obeys the green light
22 Author Rogers St. Johns
23 Singleton, in Savoie
24 "__ call us . . ."
25 Former Disney CEO
26 Piece of correspondence
28 72, at Augusta National
29 Beehive State hoopster
30 Geyser vapor
31 Tournament exemptions
33 Did an impression of
34 Middle of the quip
37 Minnow relative
40 49 Down droppers
41 Beauty's beau
45 Citrus cooler
46 An NCO
47 Less fatty
48 Knish ingredient
50 Primer pup
52 "__ Gotta Be Me"
53 Twinkling
54 Pervasive atmosphere
55 *Lucky Jim* novelist
56 End of the quip
59 Change course
60 Poker variety
61 Starr of the West
62 Genesis paradise
63 Cartoon Casanova LePew
64 They're rounded by runners

DOWN

1 Firewood carrier's loads
2 Rifle attachment
3 Accumulate
4 Veneer wood
5 Misjudge
6 Alexander or Priestley
7 Dress panel
8 Most August babies
9 Tango quorum
10 Mrs. Lincoln's family
11 Consumed completely
12 Olympian, e.g.
13 Did some wool-gathering
18 The Munsters' pet
19 Hibernation station
24 Prefix for god
25 Leisure
27 Pack (down)
28 Cribbage markers
31 Policeman's patrol
32 Chatter incessantly
33 Between ports
35 Corporate symbol
36 Skeptic's comment
37 Like some audiences
38 Decorated
39 Gold-watch recipient
42 "House of the Rising Sun" band
43 *The Marriage of Figaro* setting
44 Rapunzel's claim to fame
46 Mushroom part
47 Nursery purchase
49 Snack for Chip or Dale
50 Daybreak
51 Priggish sort
54 60 Across payment
55 The A in WATS
57 Cobra kin
58 Recede to the sea

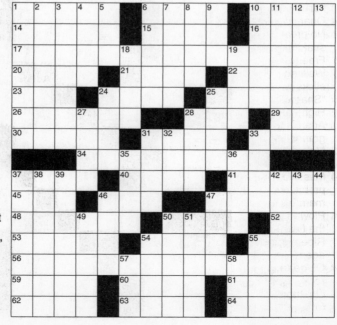

50 NOTHING TO WEAR

by Lee Weaver

ACROSS

1 Automotive pioneer
5 Skiers' conveyances
10 Poker token
14 Campus building
15 Fiery felony
16 Man of the hour
17 Concept
18 Family insignia
20 Famous loch
21 Relatives
22 Ore analysis
23 Con-game decoy
25 Suffix for soft or dinner
27 Well-protected
29 Young tabloid vendor
33 Farm yield
34 Quarry
35 No great shakes
36 Free (of)
37 Walking sticks
38 "Shame!"
39 High cards
41 Adam's grandson
42 Make a double knot
44 Massive prehistoric mammal
46 Plowed the field
47 Ripening agent
48 Oil-bearing rock
49 Lunchbox fruit

52 "Ain't ___ Sweet?"
53 Frosted
56 Auto parts
59 ___ Alto, CA
60 Bathe
61 Thick soup
62 Petty clash
63 One staring
64 Calendar periods
65 Anglo-Saxon laborer

DOWN

1 Norse god
2 Rich supply
3 Some school rules
4 Freeway mishap
5 Football maneuver
6 One way to cook steak
7 Wise ___ owl
8 Go bad
9 ___-Cat (Vail vehicle)
10 Pursuers
11 Towel letters
12 *My Friend* ___
13 Small bouquet
19 Paying passenger
24 Apr. tax collector
25 Grows faint
26 Tarzan's friends
27 Take a powder
28 Novelist Jong
29 Nut-bearing evergreen
30 Beverage sealers
31 Actor Davis

32 Joined, as oxen
34 Lord's house
37 Yield, as property
40 Hunter
42 River inlet
43 Geometric curve
45 Curved molding
46 Grad student's presentations
48 Diaphanous
49 Well-qualified
50 Beseech
51 Lay down concrete
52 Marsh bird
54 Pizazz
55 Love too well
57 Undercover agent
58 Color

51 JUST REDUCED

by Norma Steinberg

ACROSS

1 __ Sutra
5 "Stormy Weather" composer
10 Unwanted e-mail
14 Alan Arkin's son
15 What a parasol provides
16 Hamlet option
17 Shy female
20 Years and years
21 Year: Fr.
22 Espies
23 Retired tennis pro
25 "Bali __"
26 Autumn mo.
27 Television, slangily
32 Part of the eye
35 "Stormy Weather" singer
36 Washroom, for short
37 Snob's expression
41 Expert
42 Lightheaded
43 Satirist Mort
44 "__ in the kitchen with Dinah . . ."
46 Sheep sound
48 Prefix for night
49 Go one better
53 Post-workout feelings
56 Pablo's girlfriend
58 King of France
59 Food of song
62 __-Pong
63 Odin's workplace
64 About
65 "For Pete's __!"
66 Disrespectful expression
67 Low voice range

DOWN

1 Deejay Casey
2 Type of committee
3 French river
4 French friend
5 Start of a JFK line
6 Where the Lorelei lived
7 Bowling alley
8 Verge
9 The Silver St.
10 "Cease!"
11 Venetian visitor to China
12 Aid a felon
13 New York baseballers
18 Antidrug cop
19 Author Allende
24 Snack
25 __ Kong
27 City's revenue sources
28 Wild revelry
29 Arm bone
30 Fugue composer
31 Daredevil Knievel
32 "__ just kidding!"
33 Puerto __
34 Account entry
35 Camouflage
38 Self-centered person
39 Cheese coating
40 PDQ
45 Come to light
46 Street thief
47 Part of UAR
49 Burn slightly
50 Field of battle
51 Skyrockets
52 Factions
53 Poisonous snakes
54 __ pet (sprouting statue)
55 Goose sound
56 Soon
57 Swampy ground
60 Gee preceders
61 Umbrella part

ACROSS

1 Small pies
6 Door frame
10 Computer glitches
14 Actor Delon
15 Operatic tune
16 Oodles
17 *Peanuts* character
20 Couch-potato perch
21 Mil. hangout
22 Native's suffix
23 Not at all plain
26 Papas' partners
28 High points
31 Freshly painted
32 Bake-sale sponsor: Abbr.
33 Mauna __
34 D.C. denizen
35 Tootsie topper
38 The Charles' creator
42 King of the Huns
43 Dory propeller
44 Long. opposite
45 Long fish
46 Packers' org.
47 Flair
49 Chisholm Trail groups
51 Recently
53 Hand holder
54 Clairvoyance
56 Gather, with "up"
60 High-school subject
64 Shade
65 At the summit of
66 Made over

67 Ye __ Booke Shoppe
68 Transatlantic whiskers
69 High schoolers

DOWN

1 Military tune
2 Nautical adverb
3 Wholly absorbed
4 Move cautiously
5 Contemptuous smiles
6 Traffic tie-up
7 Shipping magnate's nickname
8 Courtly dance
9 Clubs for Cubs
10 Ovine entreaty
11 In the long run
12 Must, slangily
13 Eyelid woes
18 Stimpy's pal
19 Cheerleader's need
24 Missing, militarily
25 Chew out
27 Molecule part
28 *The Four Seasons* star
29 Parka, e.g.
30 Plan and direct
34 *Once Upon a Mattress* prop
35 Limbo obstacle
36 Slanted type: Abbr.
37 Ending for kitchen
39 Hurried

40 "__ You in My Dreams"
41 Country singer Tom T.
46 Motel sign
47 Confederate general
48 Exam taker
49 Was forced
50 Robin portrayer
52 Circumference segment
55 Some ladies of Spain: Abbr.
57 Sea sweller
58 Meat cut
59 Means justifiers
61 Neckline type
62 Part of an e-mail address
63 Increases

53 NIGHT SHIFT

by Nancy D. Little

ACROSS

1 Swedish rock group
5 Operate properly
9 Antenna alternative
14 Certain litigant
15 Rug buyer's concern
16 Steer clear of
17 Bridge feat
18 Take up the crops
19 Men's club
20 A little night music?
23 Where a gymnast lands
24 46 Down, in summer
25 Hebrew letters
29 Rises on a wave
33 British school
34 Reverend Moon's homeland
37 Comics caveman
38 Reagan movie
42 Harbor workhorse
43 Man of wealth
44 Bee chasers
45 Audience shout
47 Earhart's plane
50 Changed, as wallpaper
53 Pie-mode connection
54 They talk in their sleep
59 He hit 61 in '61
60 Word form for "lizard"
61 Baghdad's country
63 Goosey
64 Jai __
65 Dispossess
66 Stared at
67 Roy Rogers' real last name
68 __-do-well

DOWN

1 Horse kin
2 Onion or tulip
3 Stock-market pessimist
4 Military might
5 Personable quality
6 Rocks to refine
7 Things that exist
8 Down the tubes
9 One way to secure transportation
10 Take to the air
11 Foolish one
12 Streaked
13 Asner and Ames
21 Abzug's trademark
22 One without promise
25 Bills to pay
26 Devoured
27 File, as a complaint
28 Throw out of kilter
30 Work for nine
31 Visitor to Dreamland
32 Bride, in Bologna
35 Son __ gun
36 After-shower wear
39 More than miffed
40 Muslim messiah
41 Time to celebrate
46 Type of weasel
48 "Annie __" (old song)
49 Whitney the inventor
51 Ingrid's *Casablanca* role, et al.
52 Man Friday
54 Performed Puccini
55 Mr. Roberts
56 Pier
57 Indisputable
58 Return container, for short
59 "*O Sole __*"
62 15 min. of football

54 MERGER, SHE WROTE

by Cathy Millhauser

ACROSS

1 Sunbather's "catch"
5 Floor
10 Unwitting tool
14 Novelist Waugh
15 Drew on the television
16 __ Rios, Jamaica
17 Start of a quip
20 One of a noted septet
21 *B.C.* anteater's sound
22 Check endorser
23 __ contendere
25 Logan Airport code
26 Lava, e.g.
29 Respiratory tube
33 Part 2 of the quip
35 "Great Society" leader
37 Lennon's in-laws
38 Miller's batch
39 Role for Tebaldi
40 Back muscle, for short
41 Part 3 of the quip
43 One noted for hints
45 Faze
46 Directional suffix
47 It may hit the kerb
48 Name of eight popes
51 *Aladdin* role
53 Sleaze
57 End of the quip
60 Theater award
61 Songs-and-skits show
62 401(k) cousins
63 Nutmeg, for one
64 Bumbling
65 Word of warning

DOWN

1 Doolittle assignment
2 Designer Gucci
3 Sound of discomfort
4 Ologies
5 Expert
6 Passover staple
7 Slangy suffix
8 Gung-ho quality
9 Potato part
10 Compound in burned wood
11 Feeling flu-ish
12 "This is fun!"
13 Seward Peninsula city
18 Former Japanese capital
19 Pleistocene, e.g.
24 Show that replaced *The Man from U.N.C.L.E.*
25 Power source
26 Greenpeace concern: Abbr.
27 Obadiah follower
28 Ham it up
29 Doubly
30 Arb's concern
31 "The Hippopotamus" poet
32 Pop singer Paula
34 Baseball great Speaker
36 Practical joke
39 Eros or Vesta
41 Horn-shaped structure
42 Police squad
44 Like some glass or gas
47 Commuting hassle
48 Tabloid subjects
49 Kimono, e.g.
50 Cracker topper
51 *Gloria in Excelsis Deo* end
52 In play
54 Currency since 1999
55 Lively spirit
56 Call for attention
58 CAT alternative
59 Clique

by Lee Weaver

ACROSS

1 The whole enchilada
4 Animation unit
7 Getz of jazz
11 Canoe, e.g.
13 Ice-cream drink
15 Corporate symbol
16 Water: Sp.
17 Pound fraction
18 Mongol tent
19 Like buying a pig in a poke
22 Middling grade
23 Reverberating
24 Prepared potatoes
26 Draw to a close
27 Sounded frightened
29 Yellow Pages entries
32 Knightly wear
34 Range of view
37 Highway rig
39 Immature
41 Ugly duckling's mother
42 Winter gliders
44 Old Athenian marketplace
46 Org. for hunters
47 Use sonar, perhaps
49 Yes, in Paris
51 Romantic song
53 More cheerful
57 Lawyers' grp.
58 Agreeably pleasing
61 Turkish money
63 Courageous
64 Outlet insert
65 Ball-shaped cheese
66 Having a roof overhang
67 Shout of triumph
68 Tennis game fractions
69 Author Deighton
70 Singer Tormé

DOWN

1 Degrade
2 Method of reasoning
3 Enjoy a joke
4 Stuck (to)
5 Ages on end
6 Loafer's lack
7 Shrewd
8 Gridiron goal
9 Think alike
10 Made a memo
12 Western resort lake
13 Metal castings producer
14 Overflows
20 Singer Turner
21 Gets forty winks
25 Min. fractions
27 Chisel relative
28 Florence's river
29 Donkey's relative
30 Dover's state: Abbr.
31 Suspect dishonesty
33 Castle's protection
35 Golfer's goal
36 Doe in *Bambi*
38 Golden calf
40 Fretted and fussed
43 "Amscray!"
45 Polly, to Tom Sawyer
48 Sun-dried brick
50 Unsuitable
51 Cotton units
52 Stand for
53 Lucky number
54 Muslim's religion
55 Piano practice piece
56 Fit for a queen
59 College exam
60 Church section
62 Mornings, briefly

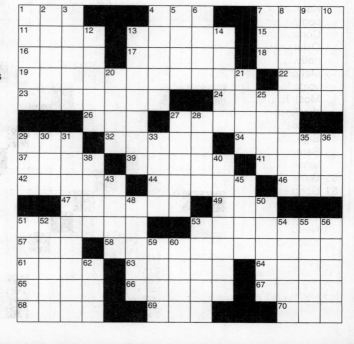

ACROSS

1 Bowling alley button
6 Wide awake
11 Assayer's concern
14 Addis __
15 Stimulate, as curiosity
16 Provoke
17 Make progress
19 Flightless Australian bird
20 Pep
21 Greek letters
22 Map feature
23 Actress Hatcher
25 Crêpes __
27 *Nightline* network
30 Fruit pie
32 Way to go
33 Racer's edge
36 1814 treaty site
39 Kal-Kan competitor
40 Comparable
42 Oklahoma native
43 Mel of cartoon-voice fame
45 Most *To Tell the Truth* contestants
47 Sign gas
49 Sampras of tennis
50 Butter unit
51 Song-ending technique
54 Vegas cubes
56 Needs to catch up
57 __-Magnon
59 Military messages
63 Guadalajara gold
64 Get angry
66 Ticket word
67 Macho type
68 Inventor Nikola
69 Actress Sothern
70 Theater divider
71 Finely contoured

DOWN

1 Track event
2 Deep black, in poetry
3 Preserve
4 Critic Roger
5 Rifle-range needs
6 Mo. for taxes
7 *The __ King*
8 Peter Shaffer play
9 Accumulates, as a tab
10 Baseball Hall-of-Famer Williams
11 Excessive
12 Send payment
13 Ooze
18 Move in a circle
22 Increase in temperature
24 Basra native
26 Move unpredictably
27 Melville captain
28 End-of-class signal
29 Graduation garb
31 Bridge declaration
34 Gift recipients
35 Not live
37 *You've Got Mail* director Ephron
38 Final, for one
41 Skin soother
44 Whisper sweet nothings
46 Whispered tidbits
48 Central parts
51 Regional foliage
52 TV producer Spelling
53 Does a barber's job
55 Name in Ford history
58 Fall birthstone
60 Choice word
61 Stir up
62 Mt. Rushmore's state
64 Govt. mortgage grp.
65 *A Chorus Line* tune

ACROSS

1 Ounce part
5 Stroll
10 Are: Sp.
14 River through Compiègne
15 Nostrils
16 "Halt!"
17 Jet-canopy material
19 Sugar source
20 Actress May
21 Adolescent
23 Poker declaration
25 "Forget it!"
26 Butte kin
29 Edible tuber
32 Devil
35 Poker declaration
36 Doll since 1959
38 Hopper load
39 DLXXV x II
40 Occupants
41 Part of USNA
42 Reaction to a mouse
43 Vandellas' leader
44 Folkie Seeger
45 Crusoe creator
47 __ Spiegel (German magazine)
48 Goldwyn colleague
49 Golf situations
51 Exhausted
53 Sees red
57 *Anna Christie* playwright
61 Actor Rob
62 Movie monsters
64 Rara avis
65 __ nous
66 Hindmost
67 Sailors
68 Leonine comments
69 Tiny colonists

DOWN

1 Dunderhead
2 Lunar valley
3 Cruising
4 Spicy cuisine
5 Cherub
6 __ *de mer*
7 Impolite kid
8 __ majesty
9 City near Bonn
10 Break loose
11 Prop pelf
12 Sonance
13 Imitator
18 Claire and Balin
22 Stem joints
24 Granted temporarily
26 Acted like Marceau
27 TV host
28 Floral arrangement piece
30 Desire
31 Yokum and Doubleday
33 Speechify
34 Not even once
36 Spelling meet
37 "__ De-Lovely"
40 Cornered
44 Shin neighbor
46 Seagoing refuelers
48 Stereo forerunner
50 Ed Norton's workplace
52 Actress Sally Ann
53 Coin place
54 "__ Lisa"
55 Casino city
56 Young lady of Sp.
58 __ the Terrible
59 For fear that
60 D-Day craft
63 Blunder

58 VOWEL PLAY

by Fred Piscop

ACROSS

1 Water slide
6 Designer Cassini
10 Italian noble surname
14 Of the ear
15 Khartoum's river
16 Schusses or wedels
17 Minor odor
19 Vintners' vessels
20 Graph starter
21 Oil, watercolor, etc.
22 Gymnast Korbut
23 Alumni magazine word
25 Steamer's creator
27 Barkeep's yell
32 Pupil controller
33 Hearth residue
34 Belted constellation
36 Manufacturer
39 Manner
41 Enjoy immensely
43 TV's "Nick at __"
44 Beaver State capital
46 Casaba or Crenshaw
48 Inc., in Britain
49 Reclined
51 Sword of __
53 *Dances with Wolves* star
56 Field boss: Abbr.
57 1975 Wimbledon champ
58 Looie's subordinate
61 Cupid's counterpart

65 Nonfactor at the Astrodome
66 Gourmet pig food
68 Eye slyly
69 Ingrid's *Casablanca* role
70 British novelist
71 Pinochle play
72 Tavern sign abbr.
73 Twiddled one's thumbs

DOWN

1 Start fishing
2 Cronyn of *Cocoon*
3 Caspian feeder
4 Gifted one's gift
5 Pipe bend
6 "Don't tread __"
7 Told a good one
8 Designer Perry
9 Frozen desserts
10 Tallinn inhabitant
11 Phrenologist's forte
12 Hint of color
13 English-exam element
18 Microscope-slide samples
24 Earth-friendly prefix
26 Escort's offering
27 Takes a powder
28 Myanmar's locale
29 Thimblerig accomplice
30 Actor Neeson
31 Went gaga over
35 Vincent Lopez theme

37 Sermon ending
38 Some checkers
40 Spruced up
42 *Patton* character
45 Hr. fragment
47 Quaff with fruitcake
50 Monster, familiarly
52 Manned, as a space flight
53 Billiards bounce
54 Missouri river
55 "Lady Love" singer
59 Take five
60 Showy flower, for short
62 Iranian currency
63 Shoppe sign word
64 Malamute's tow
67 __ Lanka

59 OUT OF COMMISSION

by Patrick Jordan

ACROSS

1 Lotto relative
6 *Meatballs* setting
10 Related
14 Accumulated, as a bill
15 Jazz setting
16 Shift start
17 Start of a door-to-door salesman's report
20 Jenny in *Love Story*
21 Did dinner
22 They form ganglia
23 Prom night tuxedos, usually
26 Extensive
27 Part 2 of report
32 Movie walk-ons
34 Kennedy matriarch
35 Sportscaster Berman
36 Sturgeon products
37 Pot-pie ingredient
38 Requirement
39 Former Texas Governor Richards
40 Goat-legged deity
42 Sprinters' props
44 Part 3 of report
47 Earns after taxes
48 Spiked beverages
51 Go back on a promise
54 *Red River* actress
55 New Deal org.
56 End of report

60 Plan impediment
61 Small amount
62 Potato pancake
63 Short dog, for short
64 Use a coupon
65 Dunkable treats

DOWN

1 Thorny subject
2 Sam the Muppet
3 Consecration ceremony
4 Aficionado
5 Make a choice
6 Type of bow
7 Suited to __
8 Witty West
9 Impostors
10 Carnegie or Mellon
11 Ukraine's largest city
12 Concerning
13 Capone foe
18 Pro football's "Papa Bear"
19 Change the color of
24 Golf-club parts
25 Unproductive bother
26 "Hold it!"
28 Staffordshire river
29 Registered voters
30 Offend olfactorily
31 They may be offensive
32 Rugged rock
33 Excellent rating
37 House cat
38 Verb's subject
40 Tierra del __

41 Is in the audience
42 Emphatic phrase
43 Cabin component
45 Extremely anxious
46 Oxygen-dependent creature
49 Large-eyed lizard
50 Rice wines
51 Carpentry tool
52 Feminizing suffix
53 Bismarck's home: Abbr.
54 Year in the papacy of Gregory I
57 Refrain syllable
58 "Hold On Tight" grp.
59 Keep out

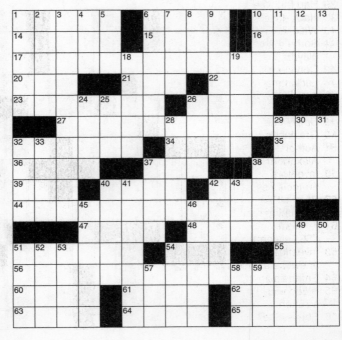

WINTER'S COMING

by Rich Norris

ACROSS

1 "___ a deal!"
4 Prefix for founded
8 Tote-bag feature
14 Slangy negative
15 Song for Anna Moffo
16 Sign up
17 1970 Anne Murray song
19 FBI employees
20 Diminutive suffix
21 Burdened (with)
23 Island west of Curaçao
25 Actress Scala
26 Krazy ___ of comics
29 Navigational aid
30 VCR button
35 Son of Hera
36 Had fun with
37 Hack drivers
40 Wise lawgivers
41 Some reed players
43 Confident
44 Lacking sympathy
46 Hold up
49 Ump's call
50 Grazing ground
51 Author Alexander
53 Inventors' protections
57 Pt. of USA
58 Drenching rain
61 ___ Bride ('50s sitcom)
63 Investigate anew, as a case
64 Enthusiasm
65 Bleaching solution
66 Social elite
67 Sandberg of baseball
68 Slippery swimmer

DOWN

1 Slacks specification
2 Hindu philosophy
3 Rose dramatically
4 Apply with light strokes
5 *Mila 18* novelist
6 Illusory visions
7 Villain
8 Enthusiasm
9 Kansas-born playwright
10 Said "Not guilty," e.g.
11 Jewelry item
12 Superlative suffix
13 ACLU concerns
18 *Charlotte's* ___
22 Knock silly
24 From the beginning
26 Boxing victory
27 Prayer response
28 Danson and Koppel
31 French landlord's income
32 Follow
33 North Sea inlets
34 Thespian's quest
35 Surrounded by
37 Designer Chanel
38 "___ Ben Adhem"
39 Hardware item
42 Ad word
43 Like a mansion
45 Hand down, as a verdict
46 Walk or talk aimlessly
47 Cyclops feature
48 Wine container
52 Omelet ingredient
53 Critters in litters
54 *The African Queen* screenwriter
55 Circus structure
56 Examine in detail
58 Erving of the NBA, familiarly
59 Wide shoe
60 Place to park
62 Trenton-to-Newark dir.

61 APPLE POLISHING

by Brian Stoll

ACROSS

1 Bring up
6 Radiator sound
10 Avoid an F
14 Take for one's own
15 "Excuse me!"
16 Nebraska county
17 Where the *Andrea Doria* safe was opened
20 Despot
21 Don Ho's home
22 351, to Caesar
23 Adored one
25 O.T. book
27 They precede HI
30 They follow HI
32 Big Apple neighborhood
36 Riyadh resident
38 Teutonic exclamation
39 Mimic
40 Victoria and Anne
44 Former UN member
45 Whitney family patriarch
46 Spooky
47 Suffix for leather
48 Words of wisdom
51 Geog. region
52 Limestone variety
54 Movie terrier
56 *Allegro __* (very fast)
59 Propels a canoe
61 "Take __ Train"
65 Yankees' nickname
68 Little duck
69 Take-out request?
70 Measure of purity
71 Specify
72 Looked over
73 Word form for "balance"

DOWN

1 Carry on
2 Roadside refreshers
3 Corn Belt state
4 *Heidi* author
5 WWII area
6 Character actor S.Z. "Cuddles" __
7 Persian for "king"
8 Succession
9 Dallas campus: Abbr.
10 Where to find suburban bargains
11 Suffix for problem
12 James Brown's music
13 Eighteen-wheeler
18 Swindle
19 Create a role
24 Bottled spirit?
26 German offspring
27 Suffix of style
28 Gounod opera
29 Visitor
31 Frank Sinatra's dog
33 Eye-bending drawing
34 Skater Sonja
35 *Law & __*
37 Streeter book
41 Guarantee
42 Rockefellers, du Ponts, etc.
43 Adventure tale
49 Dressed
50 Petro-Canada rival
53 Gas of life
55 Hitting
56 Business-letter letters
57 Flushing stadium
58 Coal deposit
60 Wheel connector
62 Zeus' sister
63 Part of QED
64 In the matter of
66 Poem of praise
67 Game-show hosts: Abbr.

62 TWO-BEAN SALADS

by Fred Piscop

ACROSS

1 Glistening garnish
6 Start for waiter or bell
10 Tropical nut
14 Chutzpah
15 Autobahn auto
16 Russian John
17 Inexperienced horse
19 Flintstones pet
20 She raised Cain
21 Beachgoer's quest
22 Burundian's neighbor
24 Milk curdler
26 *Touched by an Angel* star
27 Bandleader Shaw
29 Rapper, usually
33 Bulgar or Croat
36 Face-to-face exam
38 Air ace's button
39 Like Cheerios
40 Garciaparra of baseball
42 Kin of -kin
43 Japanese mercenary
45 Archibald of the NBA
46 Some summer babies
47 Schnozzolas
49 "__ We Dance?"
51 Zoo barriers
53 Yellowstone sight
57 Paint with dots
60 Make illegal
61 Lacto-__- vegetarian

62 Grammy-winner Braxton
63 Yo-yo mishap?
66 Short jacket
67 Like the Gobi
68 Give this for that
69 *The World of Suzie __*
70 Marquis de __
71 Brought on board

DOWN

1 Rile up
2 Launch a tennis ball
3 Get gussied up
4 "Now __ seen everything!"
5 Hoops-team member
6 "How'm I __?"
7 Network from 1995–2006
8 Distance, in Devon
9 Snow mover
10 Unappetizing spread?
11 *Tristia* poet
12 Superboy's girlfriend
13 Ever's partner
18 Third Army leader
23 Stadium near Shea
25 High-seas desertion?
26 Collect again
28 Skillet material
30 Ration
31 Plasm starter
32 AAA recommendations

33 Babies in blue
34 Reclined
35 1 for H, or 2 for He
37 Carpenter's strip
41 Onetime SAG president
44 Surmounting
48 Zesty dips
50 Pants measure
52 Aquarium fish
54 Sub detector
55 Steer clear of
56 Partitioned, with "off"
57 Hobo fare
58 Dog in Oz
59 Privy to
60 Wait
64 Unburden
65 __ Lanka

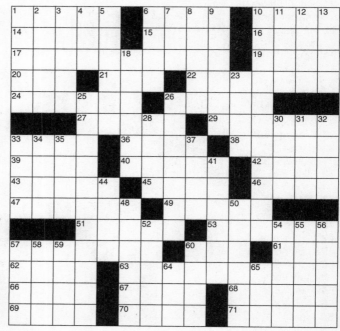

63 INSTRUMENTATION

by Bob Lubbers

ACROSS

1 Narrow passage of water: Abbr.
4 Lincoln's first vice president
10 Frat letter
13 "America" pronoun
14 Jerry's sitcom friend
15 Negligent
16 Japanese aborigine
17 Tidbit
18 Somme summer
19 Trombone
21 Fond du __, WI
23 1950s war zone
24 Hall-of-Fame quarterback
27 Haggard novel
28 Cool
31 California mountains
32 Run
34 Puts on TV
35 Clarinet
38 Breathe hard
39 Lisbon native, e.g.
40 Flies the coop
42 Pilot's hdg.
43 __ mode
46 __ a rail
47 Lost cause
49 Nam holiday
50 Homemade bass fiddle
54 Partook of
56 Solicitor
58 Mata __
59 Scratch
60 Bargain sign
61 Pitchers' stats
62 Night wear
63 Infernal
64 Squeal (on)

DOWN

1 Civil War battleground
2 Teacher's security
3 Employ again
4 Rope material
5 Moises of baseball
6 Country school teacher
7 Speak like Sylvester
8 Chemical ending
9 "Whoa, __!"
10 Part of GE
11 Tit for __
12 Fireman's tool
13 Duties
20 Silent Marx
22 Subway of song
24 Coordinates
25 Caper
26 Sidewinder trail
29 Lofty nests
30 __ and drabs
31 Cubic meter
32 Engine-knock reducer
33 High card
35 Affix, in a way
36 Troublemakers
37 City of 23 Across
38 Favorite
41 Scott role
43 Capital of Turkey
44 Ogle
45 Hoopster Gilmore
48 Earth color
50 Sudden wind
51 Hatch's state
52 It means "far"
53 __ Rabbit
54 DJ's equipment
55 __ Mahal
57 Single

64 ALL INGEST

by Richard Silvestri

ACROSS

1 Wild guess
5 Try to catch a ride
10 Cal __
14 *The Last Emperor* star
15 Joel's predecessor
16 Sunscreen ingredient
17 It may be bright
18 Po land
19 Flirt
20 What beer drinkers do?
22 Upper hand
23 Beast of burden
24 Story connector
26 Burst of speed
30 "See you later!"
32 Let fly
33 What caper samplers do?
38 *Havana* actress
39 Three-time Olympic skating champion
40 Vocal
41 What lettuce lovers do?
43 Port of Iraq
44 Lucci prize of '99
45 Branch of biology with branches
46 Small tavern
50 Michigan's __ Canals
51 Put in the pot
52 What some pubgoers do?
59 Solomon's seal
60 Hallmark
61 Declare solemnly
62 Flower of one's eye?
63 Like a tumbler
64 TV warrior
65 Hot under the collar
66 Lets slip
67 Lake Urmia's land

DOWN

1 Lost traction
2 Foofaraw
3 From scratch
4 Rowan Atkinson role
5 Craving
6 __ a pistol
7 Bomber letters
8 Get all mushy
9 Little Rhody's neighbor
10 Big top performer
11 Slur over a syllable
12 Line dance
13 Under a spell
21 Niels Bohr, by birth
25 Ground breaker
26 Oscar Madison, e.g.
27 Game of chukkers
28 Stir up
29 "__ It Romantic?"
30 Halloween treat
31 Egyptian goddess
33 Heat or Lightning
34 Gravy holder
35 Bear in the air
36 "Rats!"
37 Emulate Buffy
39 Surgeon's instrument
42 Part of HRH
43 Yahoo
45 Where Arcturus is
46 Grounds
47 Freshman course word
48 Part of a flight
49 To the point
50 Oil problem
53 Root on
54 Sandbox adjunct
55 It may be called on account of rain
56 In any way
57 First name in gossip
58 Pavlova portrayal

65 NUMERICAL ORDER

by Lee Weaver

ACROSS

1 Sacred hymn
6 At which time
10 Weeps audibly
14 Open courtyards
15 General helper
16 All over again
17 Desert animal
18 *Picnic* playwright
19 Space shuttle grp.
20 Collectible book
23 Orthodontist's org.
26 __ load of (see)
27 College housing
28 Upstairs area of a home
32 Reunion attendee
33 Small banknote
37 "Little feet" sound
41 Samson's undoer
43 Roman philosopher
44 Hawaiian goose
45 Severe interrogation
50 Giraffe relative
54 Charged atoms
55 __ Aviv
56 Journalists, with "the"
60 Become dim
61 Far East

62 Rock singer John
66 Some Ivy Leaguers
67 Imitated a bird
68 Get melodramatic
69 Mild expletive
70 Gigantic
71 *The Count of __ Cristo*

DOWN

1 Largest ocean: Abbr.
2 RR stop
3 Elbow's site
4 Willingly
5 Spread lies about
6 Belt sites
7 Allude to
8 Boundary
9 Requirement
10 __ Domingo
11 One way to walk
12 Twig broom
13 Graceful birds
21 Stop signal
22 Pastoral poem
23 Memo notation
24 Sandwich shops
25 Like some angles
29 Muscat is its capital
30 Not even
31 Caviar
34 Suffix for duck
35 Attentive
36 Indian queen
38 Little: Fr.
39 Ludwig's lament
40 __ chi (martial art)
42 Foot part
46 Getting up
47 Excessive fondness
48 Chromosome component
49 High regard
50 Put up for sale
51 Australian marsupial
52 Check the accounts of
53 Use a steam iron
57 Leftovers dish
58 Jacob's twin
59 Sailor's saint
63 Freight weight
64 Mel of baseball
65 Maiden-name indicator

ACROSS

1 Church area
5 Light beams
9 Univ. hotshots
14 Swimsuit tops
15 Israeli airline
16 Charged, as a barricade
17 Howard and Silver
18 Sanyo competitor
19 Unconventional
20 1981 Fonda/Hepburn film
23 Had dinner
24 Author Rand
25 In a confused manner
29 Architectural order
31 Fountain treat
33 Intention
34 Actor Beatty
36 Cuba or Aruba: Abbr.
37 Sp. miss
38 1947 Robert Montgomery film
42 In use, as a phone line
43 Moon lander, for short
44 Tibetan ox
45 Nickname for Onassis
46 Less cooked
48 18-wheelers, for short
52 Vanquishes
54 Historical period
56 Whatever
57 1994 Meryl Streep film
60 Croc cousin
63 Genesis site
64 Zest

65 Where the action is
66 Fashion mag
67 Philosopher Descartes
68 Tennis stroke
69 Not as much
70 Circular current

DOWN

1 Visiting Europe, e.g.
2 In nothing flat
3 Family-planning advocate Margaret
4 Bygone pump name
5 All set
6 *The X-Files* subjects
7 Show boredom
8 Hasty and careless
9 Sculpture alloy
10 Bea Arthur role
11 Canadian prov.
12 Railroad unit
13 Fr. holy woman
21 Cagney's TV partner
22 *Annie Get Your Gun* subject
26 Gloomy
27 Dieter's label word
28 Singer Sumac
30 Auto race, familiarly
32 Blackjack request
35 Cause to expand
37 Benefit
38 Angler's need

39 Skeptic's retort
40 History-class film
41 Coherent light emitter
42 Poorly behaved
46 Enthusiastic
47 Becomes tangled
49 Stamped and sent
50 Like some waterways
51 New South Wales capital
53 British jackets
55 Trait carriers
58 Inactive
59 Used to be
60 Auto fuel
61 Provide weapons for
62 Actress Leoni

67

CHANGES ARE
by J.D. Blake

ACROSS

1 Feudal fellow
5 Foot part
9 "__, I'm Adam"
14 Crosby, Stills, and Nash, e.g.
15 Lacking color
16 Caribbean vacation spot
17 Chances are
20 *Beau* __
21 Farmer, at times
22 Gets an eyeful
23 Sportswoman Didrikson
25 Acknowledge the crowd
27 Indian bigwig
30 Hamburg's river
32 Mini-map
36 *Tristan und* __
38 Items often bruised
40 Travel org.
41 Chances are
44 Adjective suffix
45 Some breads
46 Stingless bees
47 Bowler's button
49 Prepare a memo
51 Something avoided
52 PDQ
54 Buck ending
56 Hazzard County boss
59 Impend
61 Packs away
65 Chances are
68 Like Mom's place

69 Blue or green shade
70 Poet Pound
71 Stand up and speak
72 British breaks
73 Offend the nose

DOWN

1 Men-only
2 Perry and Della's creator
3 Brinks
4 Where the goal is the goal
5 Appropriate
6 Author Carson
7 Singer Laine
8 Starting words
9 Ewe said it
10 Gone up

11 Sandy rise
12 Skillful
13 Hall-of-Famer Willie
18 Ocean
19 La-la leader
24 Actor Wallace
26 Sun shield
27 Jockey
28 In unison
29 Discomposes
31 First name in flags
33 Steam room
34 Wolfed down
35 French cup
37 Pub game
39 Less conventional
42 Tennis situation

43 "Happy to do it!"
48 Baby bird
50 Actress Anderson
53 One hundred percent
55 Steve Austin's org.
56 Greeting of a sort
57 __ about (approximately)
58 Vasco da __
60 Steinbeck character
62 Flow slowly
63 Sported
64 Where Mt. Rushmore is
66 Strong cleaner
67 Bandleader Brown

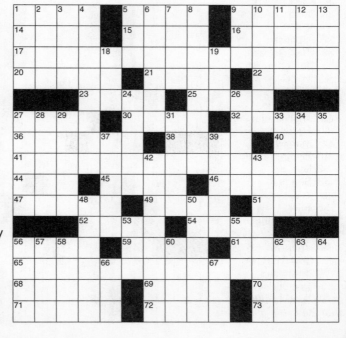

68 DIGITAL DISPLAY

by Randolph Ross

ACROSS

1 Memorable mission
6 Fixes
10 Working hard
14 California college town
15 Work without __
16 Did a smith's job
17 Going glam
20 Football filler
21 CIA predecessor
22 Actor Calhoun
23 Cher movie
25 Calder creation
27 Radio spots
30 Bessemer product
32 Pie filling
33 Opening Day time
35 Inlet
37 Think up
39 Possession, supposedly
43 Fit nicely
44 With it
45 To any extent
46 *Lunes o martes*
48 Picture puzzle
52 Itch
53 Sends to Washington
56 Effort
57 Penultimate letters
58 *Xanadu* rock group
60 Singer's syllable
61 Wall "fixtures" of song

66 Feedbag fill
67 Indication
68 Code name
69 Grain fungus
70 Selects, with "for"
71 Bridge seats

DOWN

1 Hull House founder
2 Cowboy gear
3 Opposed (to)
4 __ *for Malice* (Grafton book)
5 __ buco
6 Mel Gibson film
7 Gerund indicator
8 Deep-six
9 Bar furniture

10 Pale
11 Popular title starter
12 JFK's PT
13 QB successes
18 Belief
19 Griffin's talk-show sidekick
24 Seed
26 Pastoral
27 Seed covering
28 Opera star
29 Horde
31 Like the runt
34 Made a small sound
36 Inventor's cry
38 Unspecific degree
39 As long as a novena

40 Schlep
41 Author Hunter
42 Skiing maneuver
47 Alamogordo experiments
49 Mosquitos, e.g.
50 Agitation
51 Long looks
54 Piece of art
55 Traffic warning
57 Send
59 "All __" (Sinatra tune)
61 *Fin-de-siècle* decade
62 Shift start for some
63 AC unit
64 Med. specialty
65 Feathery scarf

ACCESSORIZING

by Greg Staples

ACROSS

1. Camp "lullaby"
5. Overflowing
10. Coarse file
14. "Don't bet __!"
15. Common sense?
16. Voice range
17. Mull (over)
18. Gemini rocket
19. Sgts. and cpls.
20. NFL team
22. Part of TGIF
23. Be mad about
24. Shoe extra
26. On Easy Street
28. High degree
29. *The Good Earth* wife
31. Moved a gondola
32. Meek's comics partner
33. The Spice Girls, e.g.
35. Ice-cream serving
37. *Hollywood Squares* win
38. Waver
41. Touchdown
46. Highlands cap
48. Shields film role
50. Sheep, to dingoes
51. Charlemagne's realm: Abbr.
52. Lacking compassion
54. London's Royal __ Hall
56. Held up, perhaps
57. Dig into
59. Macabre
60. ". . . __ saw Elba"
61. Spring month
63. Bring up
64. Heart of the matter
65. Obstinate
66. Sorcerer
67. Former JFK jets
68. Milk pitcher?
69. Dog or bob follower

DOWN

1. Very important
2. Chosen, in a way
3. Russian dumplings
4. Gregg graduate
5. ABA member
6. Stray animal
7. Accessory depicted in the completed puzzle (look carefully)
8. Sully
9. Egg producer
10. Trixie Norton portrayer
11. Grotto
12. Put away
13. Brainteaser
21. Livestock feed
23. Baseball family name
25. "Do Ya" band
27. USCG rank
30. Like two peas in __
34. Crowd sound
36. Approvals
39. Tenuous
40. Alliance of a sort
42. West Point team
43. Org. once led by Heston
44. Grazing area
45. Actor Waggoner
47. Like some mail
48. Catches
49. Ultimatum
52. List lines
53. India neighbor
55. Canal banks
58. *Kon-__*
61. Vigoda of *The Godfather*
62. Soap ingredient

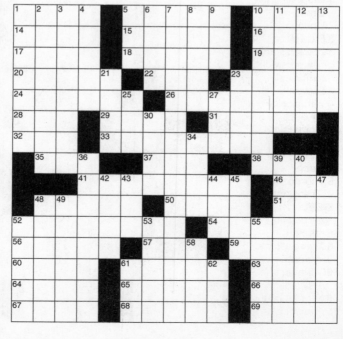

by Norma Steinberg

ACROSS

1 __ in Boots
5 Informal speech
10 Cut out, as coupons
14 Actress Magnani
15 :
16 Last word of *The Wizard of Oz*
17 Endorsement
20 Knight's title
21 Delete
22 Upright
23 Neon or nobelium
25 Wharton deg.
26 Many months: Abbr.
27 Base runner's "crime"
32 Catch sight of
35 Graph
36 Uncooked
37 Exceed normal boundaries
41 "Bah!" in German
42 Theme-park attractions
43 __ even keel
44 Come back to life
46 Ring decision
48 Highest card
49 Thai, formerly
53 Establish as fact
56 Itty-__
58 One __ time
59 a or b
62 All done
63 Intrepid
64 Get better
65 Ties the knot
66 "Land __ alive!"
67 Ceases

DOWN

1 No longer in style
2 To that time
3 Entrap
4 TV reporter Donaldson
5 Mocks
6 Diet-food ad term
7 Cry of dismay
8 "Uh uh!"
9 Economic indicator: Abbr.
10 Like some group singing
11 Affection
12 Apple Computer offering
13 Lucy Van __
18 Social equal
19 Manufacturer's payback
24 Legend
25 Producer Griffin
27 *The West Wing* star
28 Sunbathes
29 Steel component
30 California wine valley
31 Dancer Verdon
32 Practice boxing
33 Brownish purple
34 Workplace safety group: Abbr.
35 Yield
38 Detective, at times
39 Go on foot
40 Weaving frame
45 Vacillates
46 Book names
47 Funnyman Danny
49 Lawrence or Allen
50 Devoured
51 Place
52 British nobles
53 Prepare for sowing
54 Meander
55 Due
56 Silents star Theda
57 Author Dinesen
60 Dan Rather's longtime employer
61 Definite article

71 COLORFUL TITLES

by Rich Norris

ACROSS

1 Foul up
6 Expansive view
11 Floor covering
14 Earth tone
15 Foreigner
16 George's brother
17 Poe story
19 Short snooze
20 Shelley's alma mater
21 Winter Olympics event
23 Cleo's nemesis
25 Neet rival
28 Attractive one
29 Stylish
31 Painter's cover-up
34 Be less than serious
35 Seaweed-wrapped delicacy
37 Part of FBI
39 Joan Didion essay collection
43 Scoured the beach
44 Barely warm
46 Thoroughly moisten
49 Letter flourish
51 Mets' home
52 Not abridged
54 Grind to a halt
56 Objective
57 Split hairs
60 Pro __ (in proportion)
62 Old card game
63 James Fenimore Cooper sea novel
68 Roadside retreat
69 Composer Anderson
70 Fishing net
71 Mao __-tung
72 Bert's buddy
73 Four-time Australian Open champ

DOWN

1 Bon __ (witticism)
2 German pronoun
3 Timid
4 Credit-card balance, e.g.
5 Synthetic fiber
6 Rug cleaner, for short
7 Sort
8 Orders to attack, with "on"
9 Ship wood
10 Playful prank
11 Very small
12 One of the Musketeers
13 Sliding machine part
18 Anecdotal collections
22 Fruity candies
23 Summer coolers, for short
24 Open-and-__ case
26 Drink
27 Hollowing-out tools
30 Physical
32 Acknowledgment
33 Mauna __
36 __ Jima
38 PC key
40 __ *Pinafore*
41 Extreme turmoil
42 Appearance
45 June honoree
46 Like an atrium
47 Salad ingredients
48 Overture follower
50 Nixon's successor
53 Bestseller list entry
55 Car-dealership department
58 "Believe" singer
59 *Show Boat* composer
61 Raced
64 French king
65 Hurricane center
66 Flock female
67 Initials of Jekyll's creator

by Bob Lubbers

ACROSS

1 Uncovered
6 Stupefies
10 Charlie Brown exclamation
14 Astaire sibling
15 Garage event
16 Mishmash
17 Revolutionary War battle
19 Until
20 Model Carol
21 Club fees
22 Atoll feature
24 __ Island, NY
26 Gear parts
28 True
30 Assessed equitably
34 On the open water
37 *Mr. Hulot's Holiday* star
39 Poker pair
40 Pats down
42 Tie holder
43 Best and Ferber
44 Keats, for one
45 Remembered times
47 Bridge seat
48 Maybe
50 Bolger costar
52 Speechify
54 Tyrant
58 Mystical cards
61 Coin of Iran
63 Chemical suffix
64 Holler's partner
65 Conform perfectly
68 Penny, perhaps
69 Fable opener
70 Shroud site
71 __-do-well
72 Where 31 Down worked
73 Potato serving

DOWN

1 Rum cakes
2 Of age
3 Oscar de la __
4 Wapiti
5 Fiddle follower
6 Tennis great
7 Pants measurement
8 Building addition
9 Retailer
10 Teddy's outfit
11 Purina brand
12 Former president of Yugoslavia
13 Any moment
18 Charge
23 Expiate, with "for"
25 Skeet participant
27 Heroic
29 Hottest, as news
31 Fictional governess
32 Some socials
33 DA's helper
34 On
35 Nigerian singer
36 Qatari title
38 Old salt
41 Get going
46 Anwar of Egypt
49 Author John Dos __
51 Spartan serfs
53 Writer Jong
55 Word form for "father"
56 __ a million (rare)
57 Adolescents
58 Compared to
59 First-class
60 Repetitious learning
62 Gossiper's tidbit
66 Cycle or form starter
67 Flying diver

73 THINK THIN

by Fred Piscop

ACROSS

1 *Li'l Abner* cartoonist
5 Slot-machine attribute
11 Proof-ending abbr.
14 Letters above 0
15 *A Tale of Two Cities* character
16 Poison Ivy portrayer
17 Mama's boy's handful
19 World currency org.
20 The "C" of C.S. Lewis
21 Took no more cards
23 Bucks and bulls
24 British record label
27 Crafty move
28 Be in big trouble
34 Weasel cousin
35 Pianist Peter
36 Cattail's locale
39 "Outer" word form
41 "__ Peak or Bust"
42 Brainchild
43 Slopping the hogs, e.g.
45 How some races run
50 Newcastle's river
51 Questionnaire answer
52 FedEx rival
55 Put up beforehand
59 Off-the-wall
61 "Cool!"
62 Long-running musical
65 Heckler's missile
66 Edict locale of 1598
67 Recycling bin, on a PC
68 Zuider __
69 LST passengers
70 Caterpillar construction

DOWN

1 Do an after-school job
2 Granny Smith is one
3 ". . . shall not __ from the earth"
4 Que. or Ont.
5 "__ bodkins!"
6 Rebellious Turner
7 Creates a snafu
8 *Peer Gynt* dancer
9 Became void
10 Cry of surprise
11 Witty remark
12 Jane Austen classic
13 Bonkers
18 Wisconsin city
22 __ cri (newest fashion)
25 Classic British sports car
26 Adjective suffix
29 Leading man Armand
30 "That's gross!"
31 Cartoon squeal
32 Exist
33 Windows precursor
36 Prefix for way or wife
37 Hubbub
38 VCR button
40 "__ went thataway!"
41 Spectrum formers
44 Be in the red
46 Despotic one
47 Like some garages
48 Babble beginning
49 Maria Shriver's mom
53 Attach, as a nametag
54 Hound's hint
55 Chief exec, in tabloids
56 Go berserk
57 Upper hand
58 Oz pooch
60 Touched down
63 Bench-press unit
64 Letters on a flattop

74 SERVING SUGGESTION

by Patrick Jordan

ACROSS

1 Great Sphinx locale
5 Masher's rebuff
9 It's south of San Diego
13 Muddy up
14 Bake eggs
15 "Dear me!"
16 Bart's school-bus driver
17 Barbecue setting
18 Hogwash
19 Start of a diner's query
22 "For Me and My __"
23 Expression of realization
24 It's drawn by an employee
28 Couch potato's quality
33 Wipe clean
34 Metric weight
35 '59 Kingston Trio tune
36 End of the query
40 U-turn from WNW
41 Summit
42 Far from conventional
43 They do drilling and filling
46 Riles
47 Woody Allen spoke for one in '98
48 Winter hrs. in Wichita
49 Answer to the query
58 Country singer Williams
59 *Lorenzo's Oil* star
60 Redheaded tyke of '60s TV
61 At some earlier time
62 Burstyn or DeGeneres
63 Pinatubo output
64 Calendar period
65 Cherished
66 Pub pints

DOWN

1 Mushroom
2 Trifling amount
3 Tubular pasta
4 Big time
5 Shoulder warmer
6 Vilnius is its cap.
7 Soprano's solo
8 Microscopic creatures
9 Square-muzzled primate
10 Reunion attendee
11 Role for Mia's mom
12 Poses a riddle
14 Dispense, as an air freshener
20 Wading bird
21 Psi preceder
24 Plied a needle
25 Respond to the alarm
26 Get on toward evening
27 Bat wood
28 Pie ingredients
29 *Taxi* driver
30 Play to the balcony
31 Rhythmic Ringo
32 They're cracked by crooks
34 Didn't go stale
37 Sped up
38 Harry's cat, in a 1974 film
39 Carry wearily
44 Its cargo is crude
45 Ltd., in the States
46 Colorado resort
48 Supply the banquet
49 Seagoing salutation
50 Not irrational
51 Ancient Peruvian
52 29 Down, to Judd Hirsch
53 Scat singer Fitzgerald
54 "Copacabana" girl
55 Outback mineral
56 Become a donor
57 Supportive votes

75 CATCH!

by Lee Weaver

ACROSS

1 50%
5 Grain husks
10 *60 Minutes* network
13 Birdlike
15 Mother-of-pearl
16 *2001* computer
17 Get ready to sail
19 1996 Summer Olympics host
20 Quiver contents
21 The Bluegrass State
23 Taken-back car
25 Actor Bogarde et al.
26 Get-up-and-go
29 Barbecue offering
31 Barbecue offering
32 Garage-sale sign
34 Young stallion
36 Pass into law
39 Wood strip
40 Constantly, to Keats
41 Hostile, as a crowd
42 Port St. __, FL
44 Plant-to-be
46 Acid-tasting
47 Chef's secret ingredient, maybe
49 Henry VIII's sixth
51 Society-page word
52 More competent
53 Tailless amphibian
55 Lynx et al.
58 Black Sea port

62 Doctors' group: Abbr.
63 Couch accessory
65 Santa's mo.
66 Novelist Zola
67 Tara family name
68 Rub the wrong way
69 Titled ladies
70 __-bitty

DOWN

1 Laugh sounds
2 Declare positively
3 Perjurer
4 Be partial to
5 News station
6 Untalented artist
7 Workout result
8 Palm-tree foliage
9 Like good soil
10 Roundup cook's "kitchen"
11 Soaks up sun
12 Do in
14 More modern
18 Savory jelly
22 An outer planet
24 Woodwinds
26 Become wearisome
27 Biblical brother
28 Extremely dark
30 Hit the hay
33 Protective piece

35 Pay for dinner
37 Sleuth's find
38 Motorcar feature
43 Built
45 Lose vitality
48 Rodeo bull
50 Ham's device
52 One pointing at a target
54 New __, India
55 Dry riverbed
56 Barbershop service
57 Shoe bottom
59 Window-blind piece
60 Prepare the laundry
61 On the road
64 Thriller director Craven

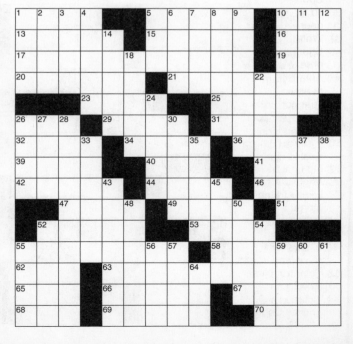

DOWN YOU GO

by Rich Norris

ACROSS

1 Cleveland cagers, in headlines
5 Plaintive sounds
10 Supplements, with "out"
14 Operatic piece
15 '50s Ford
16 Tax
17 Load one's portfolio with
20 Montezuma's people
21 Raised the lid
22 "__ voyage!"
23 Diplomacy
26 Weighed down
28 With a clean slate
30 Jet set, e.g.
33 Pig __ poke
34 FDR's mom
35 Sporty Chevy
36 To the __ degree
37 Write
40 Shoot the breeze
43 Antarctic penguin
44 Tear conveyor
48 Get __ for effort
49 Men
50 __ about
51 Scales sign
53 Flu fighters
56 Angle starter
57 Like Mr. Magoo
60 Morgan Freeman, in *The Shawshank Redemption*
62 Have troubles
65 Oklahoma Indian
66 Anchor Couric

67 Tot's block
68 Pigs' digs
69 Dance maneuvers
70 Churchill's successor

DOWN

1 Winter melons
2 Painted Desert locale
3 Seller with a cellar
4 Rice wine
5 Brainy organization
6 Praiseful poem
7 Stubborn equine
8 Verne's submariner
9 Feed the pigs

10 Actress Verdugo
11 Entered, as data
12 Obvious
13 Thesaurus entry: Abbr.
18 Columbus Day mo.
19 "On the Road Again" singer
24 Wedding site
25 Mexican food
27 Slangy negative
29 Bit of gum
31 Luggage item
32 Albany's canal
35 Musical wrap-up
38 New Jersey range
39 Tokyo's former name

40 128 oz.
41 Bring to life
42 Nebuchadnezzer's realm
45 Feral
46 Ceremonial procession
47 Checks for size
52 Customary functions
54 Takes the bus
55 Picnic pest
58 Writing fluids
59 Shoot the breeze
61 *The Green __* (Stephen King novel)
62 Popinjay
63 Had lunch
64 Split open

HATCH CHECK

by Bob Lubbers

ACROSS

1 Loch __ monster
5 Dollops of liquid
9 Kaput
13 Eight: Lat.
14 Prefix for while
15 Abrasive cloth
16 Con of a sort
18 Top-rated group
19 Hogwash
20 First-rate
22 __ of Galilee
24 Auto-tank closures
27 Feast participants
32 Enthusiastic
33 Bypass the altar
34 Lawful
36 Bi- + one
37 Broad valley
38 K rations, e.g.
39 __ Bien Phu
40 Achieved
41 Anti climax?
42 Actor Spiner
43 "__ customer, please!"
45 Buenos Aires suburb
47 Like some traits
49 Spanish uncle
50 "Crazy Legs" Hirsch et al.
52 Puts up
57 Army instrument
59 Salad ingredient
61 Show backer
62 Single
63 Check copy
64 Emcee
65 Comics shrieks
66 Stunning swimmers

DOWN

1 Small snack
2 Reverb
3 "Leave it be"
4 Scale pair
5 Sheepskin
6 Notre Dame coach Parseghian
7 Real-estate ad abbr.
8 *New Yorker* cartoonist William
9 Kiss
10 Women-only gatherings
11 Danish coin
12 Cobb and Hardin
15 Bothers
17 Twisted thread
21 Plaster of __
23 Van Gogh's home
25 *The __ Trap* (1998 remake)
26 Japanese religion
27 Blitz the quarterback
28 Director May
29 Magic-goose products
30 Primate
31 Holds, as a stadium
35 Show satisfaction
38 Singer Lanza
39 *She Wore a Yellow Ribbon* actress
41 Far-flying seabird
42 Pop singer from Iceland
44 BB, e.g.
46 Sibling's girls
48 Go biking
51 Hoof protector
53 Fencer's sword
54 Yield
55 Follow
56 Onetime Heathrow arrivals
57 "__, humbug!"
58 Numero __
60 Sign, as a contract

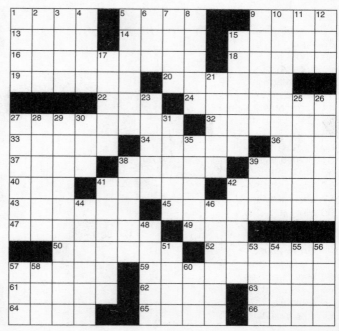

78 POSSESSIVENESS

by Richard Silvestri

ACROSS

1 Pointer's reference
5 Relish
9 Latch (onto)
13 Urania's sister
14 Church recess
15 Single
16 Hawk's weapon
17 Historic ship
18 This *muchacha*
19 The man's fear?
21 Denials of mine?
23 Syn. opposite
24 "Fever" singer
25 Dark
26 Light gas
28 Think highly of
32 Out of sorts
33 Actress Berger
35 Depend
36 Ron who played Tarzan
37 The woman's element?
41 Have a bawl
44 Make a bust
45 Wetland
49 Funnyman Philips
50 Truly
53 Canine from Kansas
54 Gaucho accessory
56 Singer's syllable
58 JFK posting
59 The thing's pixie?
61 Your sources of inspiration, once?
63 "___ boy!"
64 Julie Christie role
66 Rectangular piers
67 Golfer, at times
68 Harrow rival
69 List components
70 Water whirl
71 Slog through the surf
72 Agrees quietly

DOWN

1 Apprentice
2 Designer name
3 Resting upon
4 Of musical quality
5 The Marx Brothers, e.g.
6 Grist for DeMille
7 ID since 1935
8 Squad
9 Orbiter of '98
10 Cole Porter score of 1937
11 Colony's home
12 Abominable
13 Allen and Frome
20 Maiden-named
22 "This is delicious!"
27 Imprecise ordinal
29 Swap
30 Always, in sonnets
31 New Haven student
34 TV antenna
38 Was on the slate
39 Job estimate
40 Gymnast's surface
41 Arranged in succession
42 Failed to mention
43 Talked big
46 Cooked chestnuts
47 Continuous flows
48 Neigh sayers
51 Natural-gas component
52 Put in a kiln
55 In a maudlin mood
57 At full force
60 Took TWA
61 Trampled
62 Biblical preposition
65 One-time link

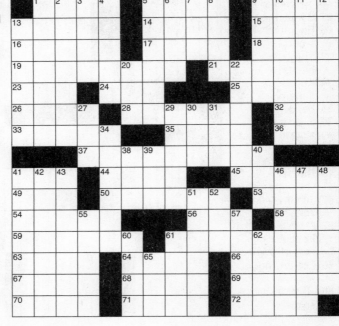

79 ROAD WORK

by A.J. Santora

ACROSS

1 Cover-up of sorts
6 HS junior's exam
10 Christmas season
14 Hoopsters Thurmond and Archibald
15 Wile E.'s supplier
16 Strong as __
17 Dishonor
18 Loudness unit
19 Amusement-park ride
20 Flaky pastry
21 Greek city-state
23 Word form for "ear"
24 Workhorses on wheels
27 Script unit
28 Engraved fabric
29 They have brains
34 Antietam general
35 Leading
39 Easter starter
40 Harsh
41 Scrutinize
43 Run for your wife
47 Johnny Mercer song
53 From the East: Abbr.
54 Part of SWAK
55 List-ending abbr.
56 Lift one's spirits
58 "I'll drink to that!"
59 Cookery flavoring
60 Sarah __ Jewett
61 Apple-seed holder
62 Doled (out)
63 Not once, to Noyes
64 Fish dish
65 Basketball ploy

DOWN

1 Foul-up
2 Riders' attire
3 Style of type
4 Do a shoe repair
5 Literary monogram
6 Daisy Mae's in-law
7 Slavic soup
8 Italian love
9 Tithe portion
10 Go off course
11 More devilish
12 Hung around
13 Divulge
21 Cubic meters
22 Objective
25 Move slowly
26 Soft drink
30 Caesar's welcome
31 Maritime abbr.
32 Bach's "Partita __ Minor"
33 Saw eye to eye
35 Apprehensive
36 Rocket section
37 Mouth, slangily
38 River to the Ubangi
41 Do __ (deceive)
42 Molly Bloom's last word
44 Church key
45 Dress size
46 Eliminates
48 Boxer's stat
49 Pacific island group
50 Salesperson
51 Soprano Fleming
52 Winter transports
57 "So's __ old man!"
59 Electrical unit

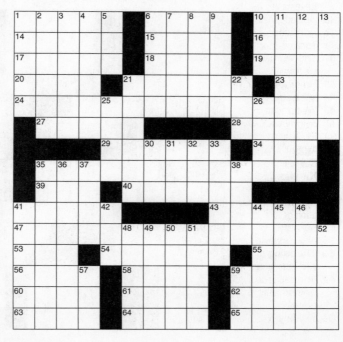

by Lee Weaver

ACROSS

1 Hornet relative
5 *The King* __
9 Aviate
12 Senator Kefauver
14 City south of Fort Lauderdale
16 Be deceitful
17 Very clever
19 MD's org.
20 Professor's job security
21 One who votes
23 Chair or sofa
25 Morse signals
26 One who scoffs
29 Joined by a common cause
32 __-Cat (Vail vehicle)
33 Business bigwig, for short
35 Finish, as a puzzle
36 Bread with a pocket
38 Evaluated
40 Author Hunter
41 Turn topsy-turvy
43 Strong Spanish assent
44 Bradley and Asner
45 Phrase differently
47 Bric-a-brac stand
50 *Garfield* canine
51 Magical opening
52 Tips to one side
55 Pulled with effort
59 Mel of baseball
60 Bread, proverbially
63 __ and aah
64 One who accepts a bet
65 Hat materials
66 CIA agent
67 Italian resort
68 Job to do

DOWN

1 Bridge position
2 Arthur of tennis
3 Getz of jazz
4 Read carefully
5 Gallic pal
6 Prefix for picker
7 See socially
8 Mrs. Marcos
9 Knives, forks, and spoons
10 VIP's wheels
11 Once around the sun
13 Indulgent spell
15 Dreamer's goals
18 One with something on
22 Lover of Daphnis
24 San Antonio's state
26 Take potshots
27 Remarkable
28 Double a knot
30 Avoid doing
31 Family rooms
32 Railroad branch
34 Jai alai basket
37 Battery post
39 Old Nick, in Barcelona
42 Most arid
46 __ floss
48 Surly
49 Baby bird of prey
52 Pigeon sounds
53 Spin like __
54 Munro's pen name
56 Arizona river
57 Newts
58 Office furniture
61 Provided snacks for
62 To and __

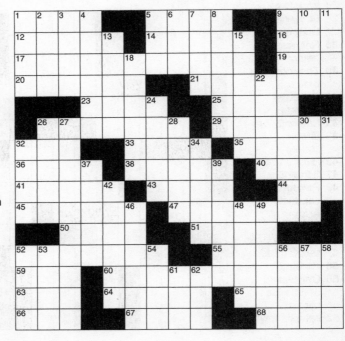

81 COINING PHRASES

by William A. Hendricks

ACROSS

1 Knowledge, for short
5 Church areas
10 Remote control button
14 Act rashly
15 Comic Butler
16 Grand Ole __
17 Do nothing
18 He makes fun
19 Frost
20 Rodgers & Hart tune of 1930
23 Here again
24 Luau dish
25 Send, as a telegram
28 Reeve role
33 Hodgepodges
34 Acid's opposite
35 Singer DiFranco
36 Nagging pettily
40 Zero degrees long.
41 Hammett hound
42 Singer Shore
43 Green liqueur
46 Most sage
47 "Uh-uh!"
48 Disorderly conduct
49 Army clothiers
56 Negate
57 Mr. Kramden
58 Ramble
60 Chichèn __
61 J.R. Ewing's mama
62 Nevada town
63 __ the line (behaved)
64 Scout's good doings
65 Recolored

DOWN

1 Under the weather
2 All in place
3 Disconcert
4 Kind of exam
5 Hopeless
6 Mischief Night act
7 When sch. often starts
8 Summers in Quebec
9 Without funds
10 Type of wool
11 Second word in a fairy tale
12 Rural machine
13 Brontë heroine
21 Bring about
22 Bambi's mother
25 Pacific kingdom
26 Out on __ (at risk)
27 Brits of old
28 A votre __!
29 Meat raters: Abbr.
30 Stephen King's home
31 Christie and Karenina
32 After sunset
34 Shindig
37 Soaped up
38 Dostoyevsky title character
39 TV talker of the '60s
44 Raid
45 __ King Cole
46 Genie's offerings
48 Speedy
49 Give up
50 Golden Rule preposition
51 Wood-shaping tool
52 Breathing sound
53 Fr. miss
54 __-poly
55 Benefit
59 The __ Squad

by Fred Piscop

ACROSS

1 Lid hair
5 Bogart role
10 Dutch portraitist Frans
14 Cinders of comics
15 Insertion mark
16 Criminally assist
17 Fun-loving fellow
20 Take the tiller
21 Critical evaluation
22 Layer of coal
25 Top flier
26 Red Sox, on scoreboards
29 Exploding-cigar sound
31 Buy quickly
36 Gardner of film
37 Truman's birthplace
39 Radar's quaff
40 Inventor's goal
44 Cleveland's lake
45 Shady spot
46 Haul into court
47 Foul odor
50 She said "Play it, Sam"
51 Trains to O'Hare
52 __ Alamos, NM
54 Proficiency
56 After-dinner drink
61 Vaudevillian Foy
65 Broadway musical of 1941

68 Texan's tie
69 Part of ICBM
70 Privy to
71 From scratch
72 Isn't straight
73 Sha __

DOWN

1 Staying power, so to speak
2 Oodles
3 Blackthorn fruit
4 Where the Styx flows
5 Chem. or biol.
6 Grier or Shriver
7 Plane measure
8 Crosby's record label
9 Moral principles
10 Lyricist Lorenz
11 Up to the job

12 Waikiki wreaths
13 [ignore this deletion]
18 Tweeter output
19 Yemeni city
23 Winglike
24 "__ mia!"
26 Innocent ones
27 Open to view
28 Composer Erik
30 New Zealand native
32 Picnic pest
33 By itself
34 Self-mover's rental
35 They'll hold water
38 Moscow moolah
41 Hamilton bill

42 "Slammin' Sammy"
43 Boo-boo remover
48 Staff sign
49 Masseur's application
53 British weight
55 Astronomer Hubble
56 Diplomat Eban
57 Inert gas
58 Castaway's home
59 Put in the hold
60 "At Last" singer James
62 Comic Carvey
63 Nutritive mineral
64 Novelist Ferber
66 Marshy area
67 Hosp. areas

83 DINNER AND A MOVIE

by Rich Norris

ACROSS

1 "__ a Woman" (Beatles tune)
5 Trick add-on
9 Cynically callous
14 Drizzly day phenomenon
15 Use as an example
16 Midwest hub
17 Basilica area
18 Interpret, as tea leaves
19 Alpine falsetto
20 *Guess Who's Coming to Dinner* actor
23 Award recipient
24 Half and half?
25 Simile middle
28 Salad leaf
30 Sticks (out)
31 Bowler's challenge
35 Stephen of *The Crying Game*
36 Situated above
37 *Dinner at Eight* actor
41 Similar
42 Have dinner
43 Barnaby Jones portrayer
44 Signing tools
45 Distinguished ones
48 Grads-to-be: Abbr.
49 Brit. fliers
50 Reaper's bundles
55 *My Dinner With Andre* actor
57 Mr. Spock's forte
60 Sews up
61 Robt. __

62 Not available
63 Feminine ending
64 Pervasive quality
65 Went out with
66 Collectors' goals
67 Anchor's position

DOWN

1 Break into pieces
2 Thick-skinned mammal
3 City in the Ruhr Valley
4 Dictation taker
5 Do a personnel job
6 Like most stadiums
7 French state
8 Kids' game
9 *Ulysses* author
10 Shout to a ship
11 Pop
12 Before, in poems
13 '60s singer Shannon
21 Knossos' island
22 Keep __ to the ground
25 Turnpike travelers
26 Retail outlet
27 Colorado city
29 All riled up
30 Part of a doorframe
31 Open-handed blows
32 Skinflint
33 Pork cuts
34 Roadside stopovers

38 Permitted
39 Tavern frequenters
40 Words of agreement
46 Upward movement
47 Doctoral dissertations
49 Went apace
51 In the lead
52 Relative importance
53 Wide-spouted pitchers
54 Move furtively
55 Smart-alecky
56 Teen trauma
57 Container cover
58 Three __ match
59 Instinctive, as a reaction

84 *REPO MAN*

by A.J. Santora

ACROSS

1 Role for Edward G.
5 Trade center
9 That skiff
12 Furnishings
13 On the Baltic
14 Bill, familiarly
15 Start of a quip
17 Band aid
18 Locations
19 French beverage
20 Comparatively irate
22 Food fish
23 Televise
24 Taunt
25 Wait on hand and foot
27 Sluggards
29 Marie Wilson role
31 __ Pieces (candy)
32 Middle of quip
37 They're history
38 Hide
39 Some knits
40 Did a cobbling job
45 NYC culture site
46 Russian blue and Scottish fold
48 Make over
49 __ *Gay* (WWII plane)
51 Mountain tree
52 Expect
53 Korean soldier
54 End of quip
57 Organic ending
58 Bob or Liddy
59 Sheds feathers
60 Walter Barber, familiarly
61 Family
62 Alice's chronicler

DOWN

1 Sovereign's sub
2 Pleistocene Epoch
3 Barracks beds
4 Eyeball
5 Domineering, in a way
6 Out of line
7 Classic car
8 Brown shades
9 Most frightful
10 Domestic beer?
11 Strong coffee
12 *Andrea* __
15 Perfumed powder
16 In
21 Stares at
23 Underline
26 Ransack
27 They have pupils
28 Newspaper departments
30 $$ dispenser
32 Whiny one
33 Direct encounter
34 Like some hams
35 1986 Indy 500 winner
36 First first lady
41 *1984* author
42 Shed
43 Fixes copy
44 The i's have them
46 Rhea Perlman role
47 City on the Roaring Fork River
50 Electrically versatile
52 Cupid
55 Frequently traded NYSE stock
56 Peruvian singer Sumac

85 LET'S GO!

by Lee Weaver

ACROSS

1 *M*A*S*H* extra
6 Beanie or beret
9 Skillful
13 Really riled
14 Actor Baldwin
16 Currier's partner
17 __ Mesa, CA
18 Louise or Turner
19 Volcano's output
20 Fire residue
21 Evelyn Wood graduate
24 Aren't colorfast
26 Buffet patron
27 Sun blockers
29 Canyon of the comics
31 Stadium sound
32 Gasoline rating
34 Like sushi
37 Folklore villains
39 Boathouse item
40 Bread's beginnings
42 Unite in marriage
43 Ship's loads
46 Leg joint
47 Refuses to obey
48 Hive house
50 Designer Ashley
52 Alleviator
53 Confusing rush
56 Cereal grain
59 Soon, poetically
60 Hong __
61 Paratrooper's need, for short
63 Nominate
64 Voice above tenor
65 Sharpener
66 Degree holder, for short
67 Preschool attendee
68 Utah city

DOWN

1 Shiny mineral
2 Cupid, to the Greeks
3 Auto's instrument panel
4 Addams family cousin
5 Came to a halt
6 Couldn't stand
7 "I cannot tell __"
8 Watch over
9 Expand, as a pupil
10 Shun
11 *Saturday Night __*
12 Russian autocrat
15 Tip to one side
22 Chilean change
23 Having a roof overhang
25 Fishline adjunct
27 As the __ flies
28 Theater section
29 Male deer
30 Poi ingredient
33 Bottle stopper
34 Wild goose chase
35 Ripening agent
36 Miss Muffet's fare
38 Spooky
41 Steinbeck character
44 "Seward's Folly"
45 German valley
47 Overdone, perhaps
49 1960 Hitchcock thriller
50 Of the moon
51 Fragrance
52 Cereal fungus
53 Suspend, as curtains
54 Young male horse
55 Golden Rule word
57 Suit to __
58 Sea swallow
62 Big pig

86 GETTING AHEAD

by Rich Norris

ACROSS

1 Not carefully considered
5 Brewer's grain
9 Lounge in the tub
14 The Charles' canine
15 Brit's cry
16 Homeric epic
17 Christian of fashion
18 Use UPS, e.g.
19 Neat and trim
20 Prior warning
23 Actress Witherspoon
24 __ Jose, CA
25 Norm: Abbr.
28 Everglades terrain
32 Wedding-vow word
34 Mil. taking-off point
37 Poet whose work inspired *Cats*
39 Uncomplicate
40 Project updates
44 Judd Hirsch sitcom
45 Huge bargain
46 Winding path
47 Hammed it up
50 Flu fighter
52 Hockey official
53 Precious stone
55 Camp structures
59 Line-of-scrimmage determinant, in football
64 Full of energy
66 Steak order
67 "__ goes nothing!"
68 Brown and wild side dishes
69 Sports-page figure
70 Word form for "eight"
71 Formative years
72 Chops
73 Office furniture

DOWN

1 Airspace monitoring device
2 Out of the way
3 Kitchen appliance
4 Bother continually
5 Catchall category: Abbr.
6 Onetime Davis Cup coach
7 Stretched out
8 Errors like thiss
9 Summer suit
10 Actor Guinness
11 Vacation-ownership system
12 Prefix for hazard
13 Summer hrs. in NJ
21 More recent
22 Road crew's supply
26 Medical procedures
27 Maxi or mini
29 Pub selection
30 Feel nostalgic about
31 Hitching spots
33 Corp. bigwig
34 More suitable
35 Bowling unit
36 Ticket seller
38 Genealogy product
41 Scram, oater-style
42 Listening device
43 Disney dog
48 Way out
49 Drops on the grass
51 Way of operating
54 Low wetland
56 Beatrice, to Charles
57 Wrongful acts
58 Shifty one
60 Bakery fixture
61 Hourly wage
62 Make a sketch
63 2000 World Series team
64 Paintings and such
65 Make stuff up

LOUD COLORS

by Mary Weber

ACROSS

1 The south of France
5 Polite term of address
9 Evergreen-forested landscape
14 Makes a mistake
15 Large vase: Fr.
16 __ Ulysses Grant
17 Actor Sharif
18 Uttered
19 *South Pacific* hero
20 Tune of 1921
23 Japanese honorific
24 Musical talent
25 Thick slice
27 European birds
33 Big __, CA
34 Singer La __ Jackson
35 Fictional Frome
37 Old card game
39 Computer attachment
42 One or more
43 __ Dame
45 Smell __ (be suspicious)
47 Jones' partner
48 Garden blooms
52 Word form for "wing"
53 __ jiffy (quickly)
54 Harvest goddess
57 Mixed drink
63 Martin's partner
65 Revolver inventor
66 Court statement
67 Seer in a turban
68 Part of QED
69 Fontanne's partner
70 Caesar's port
71 Doll's word
72 911 responders: Abbr.

DOWN

1 Feline comment
2 __ la Douce
3 Not brightly colored
4 Haifa's home
5 Grow quickly
6 Part of UAR
7 Blue dye
8 Perseus foe
9 "Ditto!"
10 Point at the target
11 Part of the eye
12 Big party
13 Prayer conclusion
21 Shaker contents
22 Shade tree
26 Lays on the line
27 Canadian territory
28 Poetic Muse
29 Colo. neighbor
30 Did battle with
31 __ Island Red
32 Greek island
33 Employee ID, at times
36 Just published
38 Game-show prize
40 Poetic preposition
41 Georgia city
44 Baltic republic
46 A lot
49 Relative of -arian
50 Discovered one's whereabouts
51 Small taste
54 Approximately
55 Rambo rescuees
56 Mighty blow
58 Director Ephron
59 Pleased
60 Donor to a school, often
61 Mailed away
62 Toppers
64 "What a good boy __!"

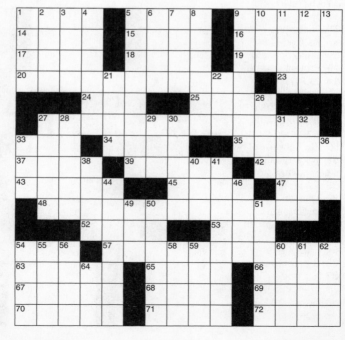

88 THE SOUNDS OF WEATHER

by Bob Lubbers

ACROSS

1 Slapstick ammo
5 Mama __ Elliot
9 Alpine region
14 Med. school course
15 Draft status
16 Lasso
17 Preliminary vote
19 Protection
20 Bright-sounding actor?
22 For fear that
23 Newsroom fixture
24 Wind up
26 *Quo __?*
29 FDR's mom
31 Bus. directors
34 Vigoda and Lincoln
35 Buy and sell
37 __ *pro nobis*
38 Wet-sounding author?
41 Ike's command: Abbr.
42 Keyless, as music
43 War god
44 No longer working: Abbr.
45 Hindu deity
46 Muscat resident
47 VI times L
48 Rough file
50 Frosh, next year
53 Misty-sounding actress?
59 Mr. Heep
61 High-schoolers
62 MGM, familiarly
63 Singer/composer Paul
64 Coup d'__
65 Terrace stone
66 Glasgow gal
67 Does nothing

DOWN

1 Marino toss
2 *Long Day's Journey __ Night*
3 Merit
4 Plymouth colonist
5 Egyptian ancestors
6 Actress Aimée
7 Ego
8 Seasoning
9 __ la la
10 Give in
11 Latest craze
12 Elevator man
13 Final
18 Penultimate letters
21 Ongoing story
25 Mork's word
26 Darth __
27 Lessen
28 Train station
29 Hot spot
30 __ mater
31 Ballerina Shearer
32 Color of money
33 Ankle bones
35 Separate
36 Biblical country
39 DEA agent
40 Tantrums
46 Workers' protection org.
47 Sea map
48 Smells bad
49 Magnani and Sten
50 Amounts
51 Pitcher Hershiser
52 Greek bread
54 List-ending abbr.
55 Actress Olin
56 Himalayan beastie
57 It was: Lat.
58 Former Atl. crossers
60 Garden tool

89 REPLAYS

by Richard Silvestri

ACROSS

1 Stadium walkway
5 Alternative to 1 Across
10 Loco
14 General Bradley
15 Teddy resembler
16 Hand or foot
17 Approach the runway
18 Fall flower
19 Audition tape
20 Repeated Shakespearean tragedy?
23 Maui music-maker
24 Like Urkel
25 Pay
29 Pizza portion
32 Give out
33 Rhône feeder
34 Sheepish remark
37 Repeated Shakespearean tragedy?
41 Dangerous crawler
42 Madrid museum
43 Top banana
44 Oozing
45 Easter event
47 Bellowing
50 Neither partner
51 Second revival of a Shakespearean history?
58 Eye layer
59 Some reunion attendees
60 Kind
62 Paddington, for one
63 Derby distance
64 Club combo
65 Visitor to Siam
66 Lost a lap
67 In the past

DOWN

1 Go bad
2 Latin 101 word
3 It's long in fashion
4 Schoolmarmish
5 A Little Rascal
6 Sample the sherry
7 Opposed to
8 The same as before
9 At a premium
10 Spending plan
11 Keeping __ to the ground
12 Lacking in courage
13 Expressionless
21 Royal pronoun
22 Photographer Adams
25 Some vaccines
26 *Good Times* star
27 Like a Dali watch
28 Had shad
29 Tea holder
30 Red, to Ramón
31 Name in Burmese history
33 Piece of cake
34 Stock-market stat
35 Somewhat
36 Plot part
38 Gig for Domingo
39 "All the Things You __"
40 Medit. country
44 Epitome of aridity
45 Self-confident
46 Pop follower
47 West Indies island
48 Asunder
49 The briny
50 Explosive material
52 St. Louis team
53 "Dueling Banjos," e.g.
54 Concerned with
55 Ratio phrase
56 Eve's counterpart
57 Actor Idle
61 Southern Italy's shape

by Norma Steinberg

ACROSS

1 Ale ingredient
5 "__ the night before Christmas . . ."
9 Kramer's given name
14 Double-reed woodwind
15 Gunfighter Wyatt
16 Discover, as an idea
17 Whistle sound
18 Cairo waterway
19 __ and kicking
20 Muted speech
23 __ *Misérables*
24 Horses
25 Add up
27 Ceremonies
30 Dame __ Melba
33 Sort
36 Beach needs
38 Verdi heroine
39 Oozes
41 Female sheep
42 Draw a conclusion
43 Easy gait
44 Boxing garb
46 Curvy letter
47 Main course
49 Buckets
51 Measure of paper
53 Puget Sound city
57 Comic Costello
59 Sennett creation
62 Nanking native

64 Words of understanding
65 Keaton/Beatty movie
66 "Over __" (Cohan tune)
67 Abbr. on a memo
68 Therefore
69 Diner
70 Back talk
71 Part of a process

DOWN

1 Flame followers
2 Circa
3 Not at all taut
4 Tie down
5 Is so inclined
6 Stand in line
7 Janis' comics husband
8 Paid out
9 Pure-minded
10 Salad-dressing ingredient
11 Painting of fruit, e.g.
12 Take a turn at chess
13 Binary digits
21 Checks for typos
22 Years and years
26 Thicke or Bates
28 Washstand pitcher
29 Finish
31 The __ of March
32 Auditory equipment
33 Small land
34 Ponce de __
35 Maintained secrecy

37 Singer Horne
40 Chile neighbor
42 World religion
44 Actress Garr
45 Feline litter
48 Former Disney honcho
50 Crosses the goal line
52 Inventor __ Howe
54 Openly seen
55 Small insect
56 Fable creator
57 Tardy
58 Workplace safety group: Abbr.
60 *¿Cómo __ usted?*
61 Takes home
63 "We __ not amused!"

ACROSS

1 Construct haphazardly
6 Architect I.M. __
9 Wild guesses
14 Make a speech
15 Well-worn
16 Book before Joel
17 Cable-TV worker
18 Vast expanse
19 More fitting
20 That: Sp.
21 "Everything but" item
24 Rue
26 Kingdom east of Fiji
27 Bitter-__ (diehard)
29 Scolds mildly
33 Sunscreen ingredient
35 May honorees
38 On one's toes
39 Attorneys' org.
40 Tidal wave
42 Actress Vardalos
43 React to a sting
45 Pop singer Amos
46 Iowa State locale
47 Roomy autos
49 Opening bars
51 "Get lost!"
54 Eye woe
57 Play appropriate for reading only
61 Patient-care grp.
62 Words to a hitchhiker
63 __ Jones Industrial Average
64 Edenic

66 __-garde
67 Festive night, often
68 Norway, to Norwegians
69 Pastrami purveyors
70 Checkers color
71 Return-mail courtesies: Abbr.

DOWN

1 Galley worker
2 Maya Angelou's *And Still __*
3 Ragtag rock group
4 Western Indian
5 Made coffee
6 Put in the mail
7 Choose
8 Place for potatoes
9 Chinese metropolis
10 Schooner need
11 Italian wine region
12 "Where have you __?"
13 *Cutty __*
22 Gossip-column fare
23 Env. stuffer
25 Genetic letters
28 Lopsided win
30 Cub watchers
31 Toledo's lake
32 RR stops
33 Handles clumsily
34 Irish Rose's beau
36 Telephonic 6
37 Rani's wrap
40 Dance price, in a 1930 tune

41 Insignificant amount
44 Big name in fashion
46 Former White House spokesman Fleischer
48 W.C. Fields persona
50 Does roadwork
52 More off-the-wall
53 Lucky strike
55 Something seen
56 Shoe features
57 Neighbor of Libya
58 Zero, on the courts
59 Fall birthstone
60 Totally amazed
65 Film noir classic

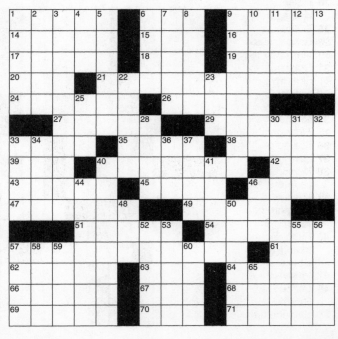

NO FOOLIN'

by Rich Norris

ACROSS

1 Confidence game
5 Myanmar, formerly
10 Some Wall Street traders
14 If things change
15 Keep __ to the ground
16 Get through the cracks
17 27 Down from Germany
18 Something funny
20 __ Doubtfire
21 Four Corners state
22 Actress MacGraw
23 Japanese sash
24 Hotel repository
26 Duke's ex
28 Something simple
31 Superman's alter ego
32 Villain, at times
33 Hair ointments
36 Prank
37 Give off
38 Monopoly property
41 Removed
45 Seagoing: Abbr.
46 Fashion industry, in slang
47 More unusual
49 Composer Bartók
50 Science class

51 New Deal org.
52 Part of a Latin trio
54 Two of the racing Unsers
55 Zero's son
59 Sandberg of baseball
61 Topping in a tub
62 Attacked by a wasp
63 David's partner
64 Outdo
65 Home on the range
66 Circle dance

DOWN

1 Put in stitches
2 Get aboard
3 On both sides of
4 Yanks' crosstown rivals
5 Gymnastics device
6 Cycle lead-in
7 Blunt rejection
8 Photo finish
9 Covent Garden solo
10 Name a price
11 Like sisters
12 Direct route
13 Short races
19 Half a dance's name
23 Approves
24 "Blue __ Shoes"
25 Bushy hairdos
27 Winter Olympics participant
29 Calm down
30 Slender
33 Piano part

34 Greek vowel
35 Jazzman Jackson
38 Flattering deception
39 Future frog
40 Traitors
42 Fox-hunting cry
43 Lou Grant portrayer
44 Ball girl
46 Take it easy
48 Ewe partner
49 Tend to a turkey
53 A majority
54 Sly
56 Very trendy
57 Los Angeles–Las Vegas dir.
58 T-shirt size: Abbr.
60 Greek vowel

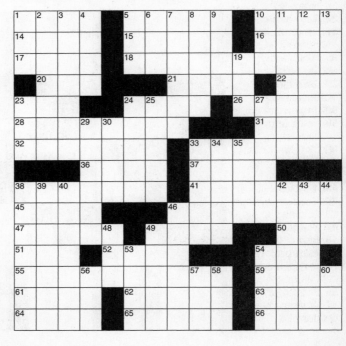

93 LOOK WHO'S TALKING

by Patrick Jordan

ACROSS

1 Landing area
6 Send to Congress
11 Toothed tool
14 Steam bath
15 "Reveille" instrument
16 ___ out a living
17 He spoke for Charlie McCarthy
19 Zilch
20 Lose energy
21 Visible gases
23 Offshoot
27 Memorable costar of Yul
28 Critical situations
29 Sandpiper relative
30 Bugs' foil
31 Actress Berry
32 Fed. pollution police
35 Hits head-on
36 Misguided act
37 Give the cold shoulder to
38 Tarzan's tot
39 Poles and Croats
40 Mother-of-pearl
41 Inherent quality
43 Annoy
44 Reactor cylinder
46 Origins
47 More unctuous
48 Part of NEA
49 They assist MDs
50 He speaks for Lester
56 From ___ Z
57 Wields a blue pencil
58 Alley Oop's mate
59 PBS cook
60 Redcap's workplace
61 Like hoodlums

DOWN

1 180 degrees from NNW
2 Smidgen
3 Snug bug's locale
4 Once ___ blue moon
5 Burns, to Allen
6 Critic from Chicago
7 Trout tempter
8 Easter paint target
9 In an ingenious way
10 Like some positions
11 He spoke for Johnny
12 Director Kurosawa
13 From Cardiff
18 Some ballpoints
22 Usher's creator
23 Sour-tasting
24 Tony Randall 1963 role
25 He spoke for Farfel
26 Applications
27 Loses sharpness
29 Have a cow
31 Store selfishly
33 Handbag
34 Assists feloniously
36 Toothpaste additive
37 Bargain hunter's delight
39 Scattered about
40 Airport-board word
42 ___ Baba
43 Dole (out)
44 Sudden attack
45 Utah mountain range
46 Mill input
48 Soprano's neighbor
51 Sass
52 "The Wonder of ___" (Elvis tune)
53 Chilling Chaney
54 Lion or Moose colleague
55 Sunbeam

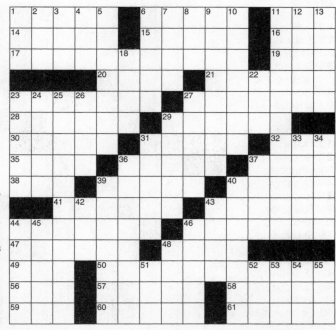

94 CAPACITIES

ACROSS

1 Brother's title
4 "I see!"
9 Piece of the action
14 Ignited
15 Sidestep
16 Dundee portrayer
17 Play a role
18 Paretsky and Teasdale
19 Pungent
20 Small community
23 Summer refresher
24 Weird
25 Meadow mother
26 *Angie* actor
27 __ Scott decision
28 Desire under the elm
31 Ethiopian coin
32 Roman road
33 Military leaders
34 Big community
38 Queeg's command
40 Norse god
41 Chooses
42 Analyze grammar
44 Word to Fido
48 News org.
49 Eternity
50 Work too hard
51 WWII heroes
52 Giant community
56 Come up
58 Author Zola
59 __ Cruces, NM
60 Flock fliers
61 Sweater size
62 Summer, in Paris
63 Church leader
64 Bed or home follower
65 Crayon color

DOWN

1 Imperfect
2 More caloric
3 Things to wear
4 *Beau* __
5 Almond-shaped
6 Produce-scale word
7 Lupino and Tarbell
8 Checked out
9 Condition
10 Latin adverb
11 Farm-oriented
12 Oakland team
13 Evokes love
21 Comic Caesar
22 Part of IOU
28 Actor Erwin
29 __ *Alibi* (Selleck film)
30 Bower
31 Sib
32 Chemical ending
33 Coal holder
34 Urban
35 Cricket sides
36 Some are classified
37 Bind
38 Valorous display
39 Things to wear
42 "Annabel Lee" writer
43 Show backers
44 __-mo
45 More improbable
46 Fly
47 Concurred verbally
49 Arab chief
50 Go too fast
53 Bit of elementary Latin
54 Former Milan moolah
55 One of Chekhov's *Three Sisters*
57 Wind dir.

by Rich Norris

ACROSS

1 Tummy troubles
6 Abba of Israel
10 Cutting comment
14 French river
15 Dock
16 S-shaped molding
17 Find one's professional niche
20 Doesn't budge
21 Stressed out
22 Prof's aides: Abbr.
23 The Beatles, e.g.
25 Update, as machinery
29 Endow
30 Video-game pioneer
31 Thin cut
32 Not in use
36 Celebrate in style
39 Normandy battle site
40 Weeding implements
41 Farsi speaker
42 The Bee __ (rock group)
43 Faucet
44 Supermarket worker
48 Make stuff up
49 Actor Hawke
50 Featured players
55 Make an inference
58 Ireland
59 Boxer's blow
60 Boxer's quest
61 Pronounced
62 LAPD alerts
63 Inscribed pillar

DOWN

1 Pendulum paths
2 Converse
3 Israeli dance
4 One of the Deadly Sins
5 Takes care of things
6 Peter Shaffer play
7 Ashtray item
8 Motorists' org.
9 First US capital
10 Piercing tool
11 Representative
12 Dodger Pee Wee
13 Artist's cap
18 October birthstone
19 Somewhat
23 Gives up
24 Golden Rule preposition
25 Hard knocks
26 State: Fr.
27 Kite appendage
28 Whether __
29 Makes one's getaway
31 Blacksmith, at times
32 Letters on a cross
33 Haul
34 Letterman rival
35 Work on the galleys
37 Old-fashioned pronoun
38 Surfing tumbles
42 Actress Lollobrigida
43 Window ledge
44 Surrenders
45 Open courtyards
46 Puppeteer Lewis
47 Spoke uncertainly
48 Closes securely
50 Stuck-up one
51 "__ bigger than a breadbox?"
52 Location
53 Turnpike charge
54 Old knife
56 Half the name of a dance
57 "Alley __!"

HOUSEHOLD HELP

by Bob Lubbers

ACROSS

1 Writer Zola
6 Hearty gulp
10 Actress Moreno
14 Charlie Chan portrayer
15 *Smallville* character
16 Party giver
17 Folk-song fest
19 Coup d'__
20 Directional suffix
21 Dracula's accessory
22 Document-signing attestor
24 Responds to stimuli
26 Derisive sound
28 Right away: Abbr.
30 Graceful horse
34 Dullard
37 Stretched out
39 Robust
40 Playing marble
42 Dress up, with "out"
43 Cubic meter
44 SAC counterpart
45 Poker card
47 Meadowlands
48 Theatrical professional
50 Venetian magistrate
52 Dweebs
54 Alex of football
58 Sinew
61 Serve drinks

63 Lawyers' org.
64 Bread spread
65 Robin's love
68 Aware of
69 Monster
70 *The Prince of Tides* star
71 Chore
72 '20s autos
73 Doctor, at times

DOWN

1 Former anesthetic
2 "A Visit From St. Nicholas" poet
3 Actress Massey
4 Allow
5 Puts up
6 Affront
7 Ebbs
8 Country lodging
9 Janet or Mitzi
10 Scarlett O'Hara's love
11 Tiniest bit
12 Nasty ruler
13 63 Across member: Abbr.
18 Like some French vowels
23 Spoken exams
25 Hawaiian Islands discoverer
27 Bugged
29 Transplanted, as plants
31 "That's clear!"
32 Razor model
33 Louis and Carrie
34 Yemen's capital
35 Frankenstein's aide

36 Commercial hub
38 Neither partner
41 Henry Ford's son
46 Dogpatch name
49 Earth shaker
51 M-1 rifle inventor
53 Richard's first veep
55 Tracks
56 Lessen
57 More lucid
58 No longer an issue
59 Arm bone
60 Collections
62 Shelley works
66 Ripen
67 Aussie hopper

by Fred Piscop

ACROSS

1 Onion covering
5 Party pooper
9 Disgrace
14 Former Belgrade bigwig
15 Waikiki's isle
16 Hounds' prey
17 Big 12 team
20 Name of two kaisers
21 Clyde's partner
22 Wagner opera
25 Envelope abbr.
26 Autumn celebration
31 Ground crew's rollout
32 Guitar device
33 Air-pump abbr.
36 Revered name in Istanbul
40 Quits surfing
42 "Uh-huh!"
43 Execute perfectly
45 Actress Raines
46 1994 figure-skating champ
50 Phone button
54 Landed property
55 Gauguin's island home
57 Persists
62 Pogo's home
65 Aussie tennis star Fraser
66 "Yes" voters
67 Rose's beau
68 Wrapped up
69 A.J. of Indy
70 Trumpeter's accessory

DOWN

1 Pack away
2 Baseball Hall of Famer Cuyler
3 "__ never fly!"
4 Webster or Wyle
5 Air-force academy freshman
6 Broadside attacker
7 "Eureka!"
8 Gloomy guy
9 Word to a fly
10 Barbera's colleague
11 "You __ serious?"
12 Worth
13 German city
18 Dagwood's neighbor
19 San Luis __, CA
23 Pro Bowl team: Abbr.
24 Ardor
26 *Our Gang* affirmative
27 Actress Winslet
28 Lint collector
29 Make a choice
30 __ up (dress finely)
33 __ sci (coll. major)
34 *Enterprise* helmsman
35 *Type like this*: Abbr.
37 Card game
38 Collect in abundance
39 Smooch
41 Bering or Barents
44 Long. crosser
47 Table linen
48 Not moving
49 Honey bunch
50 Mango center
51 Occupied
52 In front
53 Backwoods weapon
56 Angry, with "off"
58 Did the crawl
59 *Elephant Boy* star
60 Broadcast
61 *Graf* __
63 On vacation
64 "Rock and Roll, Hoochie __" ('74 song)

98 RED SQUARES

by Thomas W. Schier

ACROSS

1 *The Bostonians* author
6 Just
10 Leg part
14 "Hello, __ Be Going"
15 Role for Carrie
16 Impressionist
17 Long view
18 *Twenty* __ (with 41 Down, book by 29 Across)
20 Common Market initials
21 Put (down)
23 Hannibal and cronies
24 State one's views
26 Dreaded character
28 Sheepish
29 With 30 Down, author of 18 Across
33 Uncouth coops
34 Bicuspid, e.g.
35 Hardly attentive
36 Works on a bobbin
37 *Cheers* character
38 Cathedral voices
39 "Chances __" (Mathis tune)
40 Hades, to the Romans
41 Blotter info
42 Security Council contingent
44 *The Way* __ *Flesh*
45 Sideshow setting
46 Unnoticed
47 Eastern Catholic
50 Rumanian city

51 __ Kippur
54 One speaking collectively
57 *Año* opener
59 Basin accessory
60 Still
61 "Well, I __!"
62 Gets free (of)
63 Dutch South African
64 Passed out cards

DOWN

1 Jazzy jargon
2 Pierre's date
3 Soviet capitalists?
4 Guess: Abbr.
5 30 Down's kin
6 Kukla's friend
7 Privation
8 Put a match to
9 Sun __-sen
10 OPEC is one
11 Basilica projection
12 "__ smile be ..."
13 Born in
19 Loam, e.g.
22 Chemical suffix
25 Diner display
26 Convex molding
27 "__ Job" (1958 song)
28 Hokkaido port
29 Distributes
30 See 29 Across
31 Brazilian seaport
32 WWII losers
33 Walk of Fame name
34 Sarcastic gibe
37 Highland horde
38 "When I was __ ..."

40 1964 World's Fair attraction
41 See 18 Across
43 They may take you to the next level
44 Round letters
46 Mum's mate
47 PC purchaser
48 "__ get it!"
49 Cooled a six-pack
50 Bit of cartography
52 Turgenev's birthplace
53 Bazooka Joe's pal
55 Equality, for short
56 Altar words
58 Once called

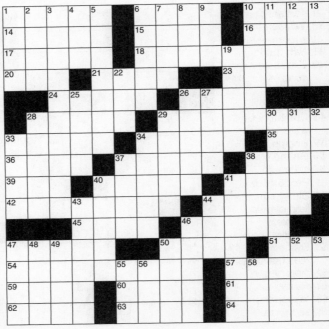

99 WHAT'S EATING YOU?

by A.J. Santora

ACROSS
1 __ facto
5 Hoosier State NFLer
9 Abominate
13 Joint venture
14 Music halls
15 Admit
16 Disintegrate
18 Actress Verdugo
19 Source of the quip
21 Media mogul Turner
22 Start of a quip
23 Manifest
27 Gracile
28 Hard to discern
29 Hospital supply
31 Molasses-based candy
35 Venison source
37 Part 2 of quip
40 Lopez's theme song
41 Baffled
43 Mine car
45 Communal word
46 Recipe amts.
49 On the schedule
51 Part 3 of quip
54 Sticky stuff
55 End of quip
59 Convex molding
60 Friction matches
62 Library sorter
63 Alphabetic sequence

64 American Plan offering
65 Scooted away
66 "As __ on TV!"
67 Grayish

DOWN
1 Truck regulator: Abbr.
2 Word of disdain
3 Now and then
4 Went into business
5 Radio response
6 Singer Anita
7 __ d'Ys (Lalo opera)
8 Jazzman Art et al.
9 Ship handler
10 First-stringers
11 Not resonant
12 Former queen of Spain
15 Walks quickly
17 Llama habitat
20 Nada
23 Norse saga
24 __ Cong
25 Just out
26 One less than quadri-
30 Early P.M.
32 Mad scrambles
33 Chimney passage
34 Ale quantity

36 Geared up old gear
38 Hosp. areas
39 Folk-song mule
42 Request
44 Theme
47 Set at odds
48 Fishhook attachments
50 University of Puget Sound site
51 Find fault
52 "__ Mio"
53 International financier
56 Teen trauma
57 Shortly
58 Two by Two role
59 Not working
61 Furtive

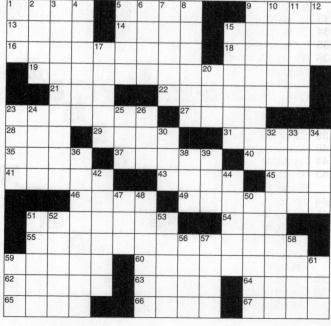

AUTOMATIC

by Norma Steinberg

ACROSS

1 American island in the Pacific
5 Entranced
9 Simile words
12 Spherical hairdo
13 Lone Ranger's farewell
15 Voting group
16 Chatterbox
18 Orrin Hatch's home
19 Much-desired Scrabble tile
20 Diminishes
21 Author __ Leonard
23 Narrative
24 Twirler's trick
25 Actress Rule
28 Blind alley
32 '60s artistic genre
33 Fork part
34 Caftan
35 Put on cargo
36 Hot alcoholic drink
37 Clump of earth
38 Locust or linden
39 Is indebted to
40 Yearn for
41 Colander
43 "... to the __ of Tripoli"
44 Grime
45 Luxury liner
46 Downhill event
49 Locomotive fuel
50 Eggs
53 Columnist George

54 Fooled
57 Actress Sheedy
58 Word before wave
59 Grand Canyon St.
60 Opposite of neg.
61 Minus
62 Heavy wind

DOWN

1 Chess or checkers
2 E.T. ships
3 Linkletter and Garfunkel
4 Bovine cry
5 Meander
6 Pueblo material
7 Papal name

8 Rug rat
9 Palo __, CA
10 Skyrocket
11 Twinge
14 "Adonais" poet
15 Abundant harvest
17 Undergo chemical change
22 Pot cover
23 Lack stamina
24 Backs with bucks
25 Startles
26 Separated
27 Consumer advocate Ralph
28 Apple drink
29 Of the sun
30 Over

31 Yields
33 White-sale purchase
36 Leno's show
40 Spicy bean dish
42 Charged particle
43 Shoulder wraps
45 Soft drinks
46 Barter
47 About 2.2 lbs.
48 Troubles
49 __ of ethics
50 Gumbo vegetable
51 Wedding-dress accessory
52 Chopping tool
55 Salad-dressing ingredient
56 Remind too much

1

```
MILOS CYAN  GLOW
AGAPE REPO  ROTE
LOSTCAUSES  ESTE
TRESTLE  DELETED
      OTTO  ANGRY
GOFER  ROSTER
IRON  BERATE  OFF
REUTHER  TEXTUAL
DON  ARTIST  ANNE
  DANGER  FUDGE
MOLTO  KARL
INITIAL  BEARERS
LINE  FOUNDMONEY
LOGS  ROSE  BADEN
INST  OMAR  ERODE
```

2

```
GET  ALIT  ESTOP
LARD  PANE  ATONE
AGAR  PICT  ROTES
DECORATOR  FROST
REPEL  NAHUM
  IDLES  OLIVES
BARNS  NEDS  NEVA
OMIT  TOQUE  ARID
SASH  BLUE  STYLE
CHEETA  ELOPE
  OARIN  POACH
ALACK  STRETCHER
NISEI  LION  URDU
SATAN  EASE  PIGS
AMONG  SLED  SET
```

3

```
RAPS  IHAD  HOHUM
AFRO  NEAR  AMASS
BRAN  CARE  NONET
BEGYOURPARDON
ISU  ARS  MOE  IDA
THEFT  TBILL  BAD
  AEC  EEL  JAZZ
BORROWTROUBLE
JIVE  ROT  NRA
IKE  PORES  GRAMS
MER  INK  APE  VAT
  STEALTHESCENE
SETAT  ORAN  ANTE
ATARI  AURA  PULP
MAYAN  DEAL  SEES
```

4

```
HOPS  LILT  CADDY
OSLO  AROO  AGREE
ICAL  DION  VEERS
SAYITISNTSODA
TRADED  SOUR  MEG
  NAN  STELLA
BERET  ASTI  GAUL
FLASHINTHEPANDA
LEIA  SOSA  ANDES
ANNUAL  WAD
TAM  NESS  BUSIED
  ALITTLELAMBDA
YOKUM  ROLO  ASIN
ARENA  AMMO  CELT
MORAL  DOOM  KNEE
```

5

```
ACTON  THROB  SKI
DRAPE  ROONE  CUT
JUICENEWTON  RWE
MLI  ABE  BEAM
  BETIDE  CSLEWIS
SIN  MAKEATOAST
HEDDA  TRAPS
ERSE  REHAB  TARE
  TRINI  ASSET
TRAFFICJAM  CPA
BRAIDED  ENCORE
RUIN  OWN  KIL
ODD  COFFEETABLE
AGE  APRIL  SPEED
DER  BEATS  KIDDO
```

6

```
SAM  BAA  ASKS
AMES  PORTS  CHOP
LANA  REATA  TARA
SHUTTERBUGS  DEW
ASSERTS  AEGEAN
  DOZ  MASCOT
BOB  DECOR  TAROT
BOLA  LETUP  TEAL
CHILD  DEMIT  ETC
  NOISES  AHA
ODDEST  GNASHES
CAD  CURTAINCALL
TRAY  BOILS  OISE
ETTA  SPLAT  TRIP
THEM  ELS  SET
```

7

```
BOMB  RAMA  HABLA
AHEM  ETAT  ABOIL
SATINDOLL  TOSCA
IRE  OONA  SANSEI
CARBON  IMARET
  ADE  SARI  WES
DEVIL  SERA  AERO
OVEREAT  CHALETS
MELD  NABS  VIDEO
ENV  MATA  LEG
EGOIST  ERNEST
METROS  TESS  NCR
INFER  JERSEYJOE
NIOBE  ERIE  EONS
EDGES  TYNE  WYES
```

8

```
CAKE  WEPT  PARIS
OPAL  AVOW  ELENA
MIRE  RILE  ROAST
BEAVERCLEAVER
OCT  CIT  DNA  WOO
SEEKTO  KDLANG
NORMASHEARER
ALSO  ASP  IDLE
LITTLESHAVER
TERSER  ASSURE
ONA  AIM  ALA  MEG
YANKEECLIPPER
BLIND  RATE  LIKE
MONTE  GREY  ORES
WAGER  ENDS  WEDS
```

9

```
N I B S   D I D   M E N S A
U T A H   A M A   W I L T E D
M A Y A   R P M   O M A H A S
B L O W O N E S C O O L
S O U L S   R E E L S   A L F
      C H I L L F A C T O R
C A T T A I L S     I T T Y
U P W A R D     E S T A T E
R E E D   G A T H E R E R
B R E A K T H E I C E
S S T   O R I E L   A T R I A
  F R E E Z E D R Y I N G
A Z A L E A   E R R   I V A N
R E P E A T   R O N   N E N E
K N O W N   S N O   G R E W
```

10

```
W A N T   I R K S   A S S A D
A L O E   N O N O   G E N I E
G O A L   B A I L   A N I T A
  T H E B O S T O N P O P S
    P O R T   O E R
S T A I N   M P H   G O B
U N I T S   S I L O   O R A L
F A T H E R K N O W S B E S T
O K A Y   O U S T   P E T E S
S E N   O A K   M I D A S
    A I M   C A L I
D A D D Y L O N G L E G S
J A I M E   E B O N   N O L O
I N D I A   S I T E   C L A W
M E A N S   S T E T   E D G E
```

11

```
C H A P   L I F E   S T U F F
R O M E   O M A N   I O N I A
U N I S   W A L D E N P O N D
M O N T S   M A U V E S
B R O O K S     R E S E R V E
S S R   E A S T E R   C O A T
      V E L A R   D R O N E
    B A T T L E C R E E K
W O O L S     A R E N T
E R L E   T I T I A N   R E A
B R O N C O S   R I V E R S
    T E N O R S   S A D A T
S P R I N G L A K E   L O S E
S H U N T   D I I I   O N E R
T I M E S   E L M O   R E D S
```

12

```
S P A   S T O P S   S I B Y L
P O P   M A R I A   W A R E S
R O O   A T A L L   A G E N T
E D G A R A L L A N P O E
A L E R T   M I S   Z I P
D E E R   R E D I G   B I D E
    A F O R E   H A L E S T
    W I L L A C A T H E R
G O O G O L   A T L A S
A V O N   B I L L Y   S A C S
P A D   B A D   A E S O P
  L A R R Y M C M U R T R Y
A Q A B A   L A Z A R   U N I
L E N I N   L L A M A   T E N
A D D E D   S I R E S   E R G
```

13

```
S P A R K   B A Y S   M A C Y
M I N E O   A R A L   A X L E
U T T E R   R E N E   L I O N
H E K E P T A N E Y E O U T
    E A R L   I V E   M T A
D O D D   E E R   E S T
A D O   A L T E R   M E E S E
F O R A L L T H E M A N D M S
T R A C E   S E V E N   N U S
    T A B   M E N   C A G E
S P A   S E X   R O A R
W I T H T H E L E T T E R W
O N T O   A N I N   L A I R S
O T I S   L I N C   A S S E T
P A C E   F A T E   W E E N Y
```

14

```
R A S P   T I D E   E V O K E
E L L A   I T A L   R O B E R
F L A G S T A F F A R I O N A
R E V E I L L E   N O L E S
Y E S   I E L   A I R E
    R N S   O R B   S T A S
S C R A G   M A C A O   R P I
T H E P U L I T E R P R I E S
O O T   P I N E D   T A B R I
P O E T   O E R   L I N
    W A N D   A I M   W A S
T H E N I   C L A I M A N T
Q U E E N E L I A B E T H I I
A L B E E   A R I L   N O E L
T E E R S   G E N E   S O R T
```

15

```
R O B S   R A B B I   L A L A
O P A H   O R L O N   A J A X
S E C O N D C O A T   M A Z E
S C H W A   O T T O   B R E D
      U M P   T E C
C A P E O F G O O D H O P E
N A M   D E A N   T O R R E
A V O N   S I Z E S   P A I L
R I C E S   G E N E   T O Y
C L O A K A N D D A G G E R
    R I D   S I R
S K I M   O L L A   L O O S E
H A R I   B O O K J A C K E T
E Y E S   E L L I E   E R I C
M O S S   S L A N T   R A S H
```

16

```
L O G E S   M A T   A M I S S
A R E N T   E R R   M A R A T
P E N T A   R E A   O S A G E
P O L I T I C A L A R E N A
    R E N   E V E R
B A B E   C A G E S   A S E A
E D A   B A E R   O T T E R
H O L D E N C A U L F I E L D
A R S O N   S P O T   N E E
N E A L   B A S I N   C O R N
    E R A S   G P A
I N D U S T R I A L P A R K
O D E O N   R E C   O L L I E
C L O U T   A G O   P E A C E
T E N T S   L O N   S T R O P
```

17

```
E L L A   C L A I M   N A S H
R O A R   L O R N E   O J A I
G U M C H E W I N G   T A K E
O D E   A R E A   A L E X I S
    D I G S   S T O P
R O S A R Y   Q U O T A B L E
O K A Y S   D U R N   S L A V
Y A R D   T O I L S   S A N E
A P A R   I N D Y   W I Z E N
L I N E A G E S   E R N E S T
    A S H E   B R I G
P R O M P T   T A U T   F O E
L E V I   W H I S P E R I N G
O P E N   A U D I T   O L E G
W O N G   D R E S S   T E S S
```

18

```
S A I D   I R M A   G N A T
U S M A   T U R B O   L U G E
E T A B I G M E A L   A Y E S
R E D B L O O D   E S C O R T
S P E L L E R   A S H E R
E S S   L U T E   K I D
G Y P S   N O T R E   E V A
R O I   R H O B O A T   R E F
A G A   H O L E S   P S S T
M I L   E S T S   C A R
  A B A T E   R O B E R T S
B E M U S E   S O L U T I O N
A D O S   L E T O U T A P S I
C E D E   S P A S M   P E E P
O N E S   A T T N   E R A S
```

19

```
A U D I   W O V E   C P L
S N A G   I R O N W A R E
I F Y O U D O N T K N O W
A N O   R A T   L T D
S I L K   W H E R E Y O U R E
I N D I A   S N E E   N C A A
N E S T S   T A R T   T N T
    H E A D E D Y O U
L A B   A L A R   U R B A N
A S A P   A W E D   R I L L E
W I L L W I N D U P   S E G O
C U E   L O P   S I N
S O M E P L A C E E L S E
I N E D I B L E   E Y E R
C Y D   P S S T   R E D S
```

20

```
S A G S   L A N A   P A N E L
O G R E   I L E S   E R I C A
D O A S   N I G H T L I G H T
O R N A T E   R O I L   H O E
M A D M A D   I T E M S
  S E R U M   R E C E D E
M S T   P O D   S L I V E R
A W A R D   D U B   L O E S S
Z A N I E S   D A H   N I T
E N D M A N   R O S E S
  A D O R E   T O M T O M
S H E   H O O D   S L E E V E
H O D G E P O D G E   E V I L
I N D I A   S I M A   R E N E
M E A N D   T E S T   S N E E
```

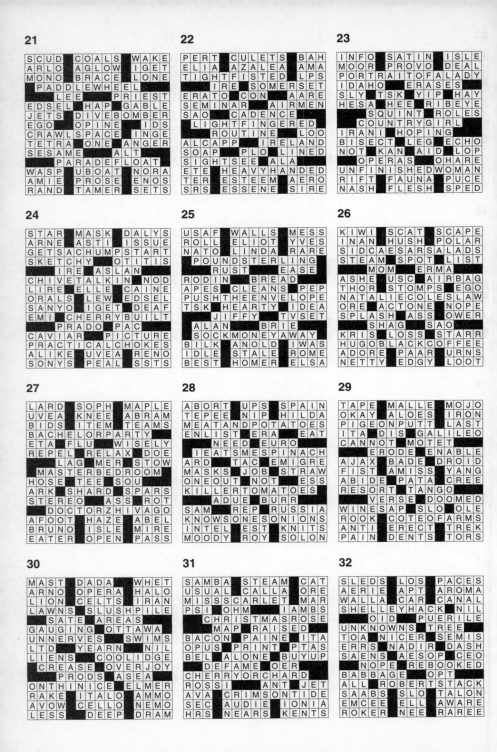

21

S	C	U	D		C	O	A	L	S		W	A	K	E
A	R	L	O		A	G	L	O	W		I	G	E	T
M	O	N	O		B	R	A	C	E		L	O	N	E
	P	A	D	D	L	E	W	H	E	E	L			
			L	E	E				P	R	I	E	S	T
E	D	S	E	L		H	A	P		G	A	B	L	E
J	E	T	S		D	I	V	E	B	O	M	B	E	R
E	G	O		O	P	I	N	E			I	D	S	
C	R	A	W	L	S	P	A	C	E			I	N	G	E
T	E	T	R	A		O	N	E		A	N	G	E	R
S	E	S	A	M	E			A	L	T				
			P	A	R	A	D	E	F	L	O	A	T	
W	A	S	P		U	B	O	A	T		N	O	R	A
A	M	I	E		P	R	O	S	E		E	N	O	S
R	A	N	D		T	A	M	E	R		S	E	T	S

22

P	E	R	T		C	U	L	E	T	S		B	A	H
E	L	I	A		A	Z	A	L	E	A		A	M	A
T	I	G	H	T	F	I	S	T	E	D		L	P	S
		I	R	E				S	O	M	E	R	S	E	T
E	R	A	T	O		C	O	N			A	A	R	E
S	E	M	I	N	A	R			A	I	R	M	E	N
S	A	O		C	A	D	E	N	C	E				
	L	I	G	H	T	F	I	N	G	E	R	E	D	
			R	O	U	T	I	N	E		L	O	O	
A	L	C	A	P	P			I	R	E	L	A	N	D
S	O	A	P		P	L	O		L	I	N	E	D	
S	I	G	H	T	S	E	E		A	L	A			
E	T	E		H	E	A	V	Y	H	A	N	D	E	D
T	E	R		E	S	T	E	E	M		A	E	R	O
S	R	S		E	S	S	E	N	E		S	I	R	E

23

I	N	F	O		S	A	T	I	N		I	S	L	E
M	O	O	R		P	R	O	V	O		D	E	A	L
P	O	R	T	R	A	I	T	O	F	A	L	A	D	Y
I	D	A	H	O			E	R	A	S	E	S		
S	L	Y		T	S	K		Y	I	P		H	A	Y
H	E	S	A		H	E	E		R	I	B	E	Y	E
			S	Q	U	I	N	T		R	O	L	E	S
	C	O	U	N	T	R	Y	G	I	R	L			
I	R	A	N	I		H	O	P	I	N	G			
B	I	S	E	C	T		L	E	G		E	C	H	O
N	O	T		K	A	N		A	I	D		L	O	P
	O	P	E	R	A	S			O	H	A	R	E	
U	N	F	I	N	I	S	H	E	D	W	O	M	A	N
R	I	F	T		F	A	U	N	A		P	U	C	E
N	A	S	H		F	L	E	S	H		S	P	E	D

24

S	T	A	R		M	A	S	K		D	A	L	Y	S
A	R	N	E		A	S	T	I		I	S	S	U	E
G	E	T	S	A	C	H	U	M	P	S	T	A	R	T
S	K	E	T	C	H	Y		O	T	I	T	I	S	
			I	R	E		A	S	L	A	N			
C	H	I	V	E	T	A	L	K	I	N		N	O	D
L	I	R	E		E	L	L	E		C	A	I	N	E
O	R	A	L	S		L	E	W		E	D	S	E	L
S	A	N	Y	O		I	G	E	T		D	E	A	F
E	M	I		C	H	E	R	R	Y	B	U	I	L	T
			P	R	A	D	O		P	A	C			
C	A	V	I	A	R			P	I	C	T	U	R	E
P	R	A	C	T	I	C	A	L	C	H	O	K	E	S
A	L	I	K	E		U	V	E	A		R	E	N	O
S	O	N	Y	S		P	E	A	L		S	S	T	S

25

U	S	A	F		W	A	L	L	S		M	E	S	S
R	O	L	L		E	L	I	O	T		Y	V	E	S
N	A	T	O		L	I	N	D	A		R	A	R	E
	P	O	U	N	D	S	T	E	R	L	I	N	G	
			R	U	S	T			E	A	S	E		
R	O	D	I	N			B	R	E	A	D			
A	P	E	S		C	L	E	A	N	S		P	E	P
P	U	S	H	T	H	E	E	N	V	E	L	O	P	E
T	S	K		H	E	A	R	T	Y		I	D	E	A
			J	I	F	F	Y			T	V	S	E	T
A	L	A	N		B	R	I	E						
S	O	C	K	M	O	N	E	Y	A	W	A	Y		
B	I	L	K		A	N	O	L	D		I	W	A	S
I	D	L	E		S	T	A	L	E		R	O	M	E
B	E	S	T		H	O	M	E	R		E	L	S	A

26

K	I	W	I		S	C	A	T		S	C	A	P	E
I	N	A	N		H	U	S	H		P	O	L	A	R
S	I	D	C	A	E	S	A	R	S	A	L	A	D	S
S	T	E	A	M		S	P	O	T		L	I	S	T
			M	O	M		E	R	M	A				
A	S	H	E		U	S	C		A	I	R	B	A	G
T	H	O	R		S	T	O	M	P	S		E	G	O
N	A	T	A	L	I	E	C	O	L	E	S	L	A	W
O	R	E		A	C	T	O	N	E		N	O	P	E
S	P	L	A	S	H		A	S	S		O	W	E	R
			S	H	A	G			S	A	O			
K	R	I	S		L	O	S	S		S	T	A	R	R
H	U	G	O	B	L	A	C	K	C	O	F	F	E	E
A	D	O	R	E		P	A	A	R		U	R	N	S
N	E	T	T	Y		E	D	G	Y		L	O	O	T

27

L	A	R	D		S	O	P	H		M	A	P	L	E
U	V	E	A		K	N	E	E		A	B	R	A	M
B	I	D	S		I	T	E	M		T	E	A	M	S
B	A	C	H	E	L	O	R	P	A	R	T	Y		
E	T	A		F	L	U			W	I	S	E	L	Y
R	E	P	E	L		R	E	L	A	X		D	O	E
			L	A	G		M	E	R		S	T	O	W
	M	A	S	T	E	R	B	E	D	R	O	O	M	
H	O	S	E		T	E	E			S	O	U		
A	R	K		S	H	A	R	D		S	P	A	R	S
S	T	E	R	E	O			A	S	S		R	O	T
			D	O	C	T	O	R	Z	H	I	V	A	G	O
A	F	O	O	T		H	A	Z	E		A	B	E	L
B	R	U	N	O		I	S	L	E		M	I	R	E
E	A	T	E	R		O	P	E	N		P	A	S	S

28

A	B	O	R	T		U	P	S		S	P	A	I	N
T	E	P	E	E		N	I	P		H	I	L	D	A
M	E	A	T	A	N	D	P	O	T	A	T	O	E	S
E	N	L	I	S	T		E	R	A			E	A	T
			N	E	E	D		E	U	R	O			
I	E	A	T	S	M	E	S	P	I	N	A	C	H	
A	R	D			T	A	C		E	M	I	G	R	E
M	A	S	K	S		J	O	B		S	T	R	A	W
O	N	E	O	U	T		N	O	T			E	S	S
		K	I	L	L	E	R	T	O	M	A	T	O	E	S
	A	D	U	E			B	U	R	R				
S	A	M		R	E	P		R	U	S	S	I	A	
K	N	O	W	S	O	N	E	S	O	N	I	O	N	S
I	N	T	E	L		E	S	T		K	N	I	T	S
M	O	O	D	Y		R	O	Y		S	O	L	O	N

29

T	A	P	E		M	A	L	L	E		M	O	J	O
O	K	A	Y		A	L	O	E	S		I	R	O	N
P	I	G	E	O	N	P	U	T	T		L	A	S	T
I	T	A		D	I	S		G	A	L	I	L	E	O
C	A	N	N	O	T		M	O	T	E	T			
			E	R	O	D	E			E	N	A	B	L	E
A	J	A	X		B	A	D	E			D	R	O	I	D
F	I	S	T		A	M	I	S	S			Y	A	N	G
A	B	I	D	E		P	A	T	A		C	R	E	E
R	E	S	O	R	T			T	A	N	G	O		
			V	E	R	S	E		D	O	O	M	E	D
W	I	N	E	S	A	P		S	L	O		O	L	E
R	O	O	K		C	O	T	E	O	F	F	A	R	M	S
A	N	T	I		E	R	E	C	T		T	R	E	K
P	A	I	N		D	E	N	T	S		T	O	R	S

30

M	A	S	T		D	A	D	A		W	H	E	T	
A	R	N	O		O	P	E	R	A		H	A	L	O
L	I	O	N		C	E	L	T	S		I	R	A	N
L	A	W	N	S		S	L	U	S	H	P	I	L	E
			S	A	T	E		A	R	E	A	S		
G	A	U	G	I	N	G		O	T	T	A	W	A	
U	N	N	E	R	V	E	S		S	W	I	M	S	
L	T	D		Y	E	A	R	N		N	I	L		
L	I	E	N	S		C	O	O	L	I	D	G	E	
	C	R	E	A	S	E		O	V	E	R	J	O	Y
			P	R	O	D	S		A	S	E	A		
O	N	T	H	I	N	I	C	E		E	L	M	E	R
R	A	K	E		I	T	A	L	O		A	M	M	O
A	V	O	W		C	E	L	L	O			N	E	M	O
L	E	S	S			D	E	E	P		D	R	A	M

31

S	A	M	B	A		S	T	E	A	M		C	A	T
U	S	U	A	L		C	A	L	L	A		O	R	E
M	I	S	S	S	C	A	R	L	E	T		M	A	R
P	S	I		O	H	M			I	A	M	B	S	
			C	H	R	I	S	T	M	A	S	R	O	S	E
		M	A	P		R	A	I	S	E	D			
B	A	C	O	N		P	A	I	N	E		I	T	A
O	P	U	S		P	R	I	N	T		P	T	A	S
B	E	L		A	L	O	N	E		B	U	Y	U	P
	D	E	F	A	M	E			O	E	R			
C	H	E	R	R	Y	O	R	C	H	A	R	D		
R	O	S	S	I		A	N	T		J	E	T		
A	V	A		C	R	I	M	S	O	N	T	I	D	E
S	E	C		A	U	D	I	E		I	O	N	I	A
H	R	S		N	E	A	R	S		K	E	N	T	S

32

S	L	E	D	S		L	O	S		P	A	C	E	S
A	E	R	I	E		A	P	T		A	R	O	M	A
W	A	L	L	A		C	A	R		C	A	N	A	L
S	H	E	L	L	E	Y	H	A	C	K		N	I	L
			O	I	D		P	U	E	R	I	L	E	
U	N	K	N	O	W	N	S		T	R	E	E		
T	O	A		N	I	C	E	R		S	E	M	I	S
E	R	R	S		N	A	D	I	R		D	A	S	H
S	A	E	N	S		A	E	S	O	P		C	E	O
			N	O	P	E		R	E	B	O	O	K	E	D
B	A	B	B	A	G	E			O	P	T			
A	L	L		R	O	B	E	R	T	S	T	A	C	K
S	A	A	B	S		S	L	O		T	A	L	O	N
E	M	C	E	E		E	L	L		A	W	A	R	E
R	O	K	E	R		N	E	E		R	A	R	E	E

33

```
BAIT . ODDS . URBAN
ARCH . LARA . SHANE
STEELDRUM . SURGE
. GOINGAT . MRED .
METROS . ROBBERS
ERIE . HOB . ELAL
ANNAS . VERDI . HSI
DEPTH . ERA . GROAN
SSA . ABNER . HEURE
NERO . TET . TSAR
REALISM . WERENT
. ELLA . CARIOCA .
HELIO . GUTBUCKET
ANENT . MMII . TITO
BAYES . ASST . SNAP
```

34

```
CLOG . MAMAS . AJAX
RIDE . ABASH . DARE
AVON . TUTTI . INKS
MEREPITTANCE . .
. . TESS . GOUDAS
ESPIES . SLR . ACE
CHICKENFEED . MCI
LETS . OFA . EARS
ALI . TRIFLINGSUM
IVE . HER . COOKES
REDSEA . SIAM . .
. POCKETCHANGE
STAR . TOTAL . NELL
IOWA . ELATE . IRES
RELY . DALES . AONE
```

35

```
NAOMI . RACK . ROSA
OFTEN . OLLA . EKED
STIRS . OPAL . PLED
. SETONONESEARS
. . . ABE . SON . .
BEALLEYES . OTTER
RARELY . ATEN . ORE
ASEA . ESTES . ARIA
YEN . BRAE . TENSED
SLATE . ONTHENOSE
. . ITS . EER . . .
MOUTHWATERING .
URSA . ALIT . EARLS
TEEN . YORE . SPIEL
TORS . SUER . TANGO
```

36

```
ABCS . SHOP . STPAT
BELT . TELL . CORGI
ALIE . AREA . OLIOS
SUPPORTSYSTEM .
EGO . NEZ . UTTERS
DANCE . FANS . VIE
. LAPSING . CAGE .
. COLUMNTOTAL .
BEAT . TONEDUP .
ART . COGS . NOHIT
NASSAU . AMI . USA
. POSTOFFICEBOX
CRAFT . DATA . MCLI
ANWAR . ELEM . MADE
BASSO . SARI . APES
```

37

```
ALGA . SCARF . NOTE
LEON . ULNAR . OMEN
BANG . NINNY . WANT
SPEEDBOAT . CANER
. LIE . SOLIDITY
ALMANAC . TRA . .
LEE . MOTORCYCLE
MAMAS . BAG . ASHOT
SNOWMOBILE . AVA
. AID . EXCUSES .
BEWILDER . PUN .
ORATE . DUNEBUGGY
GIGI . ESSEN . SIRE
ECON . MESAS . ELAN
YANG . SLOPE . DABS
```

38

```
FENS . PASS . DECAL
ARIA . OMIT . ELATE
DANLBOONE . NAPES
STATED . NOTIN . .
. . . ALTA . DANCES
BABBLERS . ETERNE
AROSE . APPLE . UTA
LISA . IDEAL . SNIT
TAN . ERECT . SACRE
INSOLE . THRASHER
CAMDEN . SEAT . . .
. ADMEN . TINGED .
HITME . AMOSNANDY
OCEAN . DODO . MADE
TISNT . AMEN . ERAS
```

39

```
MARZIPAN . REMAPS
ALIENATE . EVILLY
BIGNAMES . EONIAN
LOG . NELSONEDDY
ETES . LIEUT . TAMP
YODH . AESIR . ODAS
. USSR . SYD . ETS
ABATE . . . INSET
BOP . EST . SMEE .
CLIP . HASTE . ERIS
SOAR . ARTEL . RANT
. GREGMORRIS . THO
ENISLE . ANNASTEN
PASTOR . MEDICARE
TSTOPS . PRALINES
```

40

```
HOPS . TRILL . SHEB
OKIE . RENEE . TONE
WALTZINGMATILDA
EYE . EPEE . INEED
. CROW . NECTARY
METHOD . BOLTS . .
ACRE . GENOA . MAA
CHARLESTONCHEWS
KOP . AQUAS . ALAI
. YOUIS . WENDYS .
APPETIT . TOAD . .
TOILS . DONS . MAS
PEPPERMINTTWIST
ATEE . AIRED . ACHY
REDD . NITRO . CHEX
```

41

```
BLORE . SHISH . ACT
LINEN . TODAY . SAO
TUESDAYWELD . PRO
. RASP . TALE . IST
AEON . PROSE . TREE
PRUDHOE . SPREAD
ENS . OSES . LAST .
. . JOEFRIDAY . .
STET . ADEN . OAT
STRESS . OCTANTS
PEER . HANSA . VALE
ARA . ARLO . FRAN
ROT . BILLYSUNDAY
TIE . EVITA . STORE
ADD . RESET . TINTS
```

42

```
GAS . STEAM . CBER
EPI . COSTA . THEME
LOGROLLER . AIMED
SNARE . ALEXCORD
STEWED . MON . AGE
OLD . DOW . DOWNER
PEON . INTOTO . .
. NATALIEWOOD .
. VORTEX . LION .
IMPEND . TLC . SKI
NEO . OUR . ELICIT
SAWHORSE . AARON
OGDEN . EMANUELAX
LEERS . RIDES . OWE
ERRS . STORE . RAD
```

43

```
RASTA . PATS . TRAP
ORLON . EDIT . AIDA
STANDANDDELIVER
ASTERN . LYRE . ELI
. REESE . NANTES
BBC . AMP . HONE .
ARIA . IOTA . EVADE
SITBACKANDRELAX
SMEAR . EDDY . RUDE
. TIES . EER . MAS
WALESA . ELVES .
ARI . TRAM . ASTAGE
LIEDOWNONTHEJOB
LEGO . INTO . INAIR
SLEW . GOER . PORTO
```

44

```
LIMIT . AGOG . IVAN
IRENE . LUNA . MIME
MILAN . ARES . MEET
ADDRESSUNKNOWN
. . UMA . DEER . .
PRETERIT . TATARS
AOL . NACHO . ABUT
PUSHTHEENVELOPE
ASIA . DICES . WEE
STERNA . RESTYLED
. . DIRT . TIA . .
RUBBERSTAMPING
NOVA . NATO . APRIL
ABEL . ALUM . TEMPE
PEAL . SADE . ERASE
```

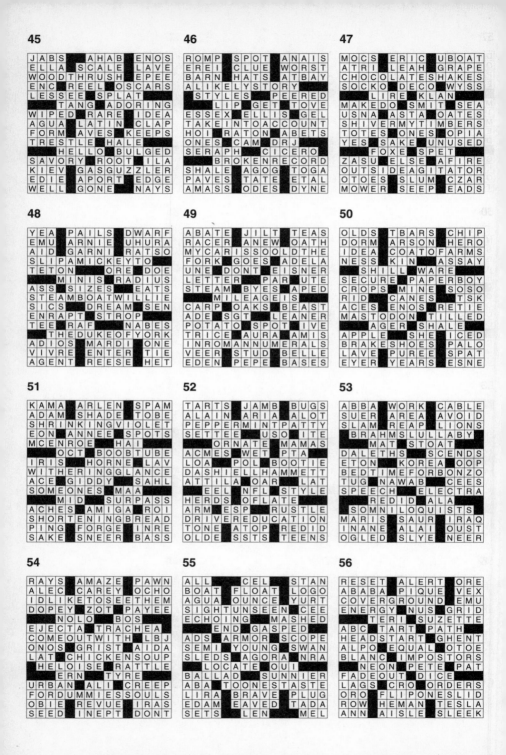

45

```
J A B S   A H A B   E N O S
E L L A   S C A L E   L A V E
W O O D T H R U S H   E P E E
E N C   R E E L   O S C A R S
L E S S E E   S P L A T
      T A N G   A D O R I N G
W I P E D   R A R E   I D E A
A G U A   L A T I N   C L A P
F O R M   A V E S   K E E P S
T R E S T L E   H A L E
      H E L L O   B U L G E D
S A V O R Y   R O O T   I L A
K I E V   G A S G U Z Z L E R
E D I E   A P O R T   E D G E
W E L L   G O N E   N A Y S
```

46

```
R O M P   S P O T   A N A I S
E R E I   C L U E   W O R S T
B A R N   H A T S   A T B A Y
A L I K E L Y S T O R Y
      S T Y L E S   P E E R E D
L I P   G E T   T O V E
E S S E X   E L L I S   G E L
T A K E I N T O A C C O U N T
H O I   R A T O N   A B E T S
O N E S   C A M   D R J
S E R A P H   C I C E R O
      B R O K E N R E C O R D
S H A L E   A G O G   T O G A
P A V E S   T A T E   E T A L
A M A S S   O D E S   D Y N E
```

47

```
M O C S   E R I C   U B O A T
A T R I   L E A H   G R A P E
C H O C O L A T E S H A K E S
S O C K O   D E C O   W Y S S
      L I R E   K L A N
M A K E D O   S M I T   S E A
U S N A   A S T A   O A T E S
S H I V E R M Y T I M B E R S
T O T E S   O N E S   O P I A
Y E S   S A K E   U N U S E D
      F O X E   S P E T
Z A S U   E L S E   A F I R E
O U T S I D E A G I T A T O R
O T O E S   S L U M   C Z A R
M O W E R   S E E P   E A D S
```

48

```
Y E A   P A I L S   D W A R F
E M U   A R N I E   U H U R A
A I D   G A R N I   R A T S O
S L I P A M I C K E Y T O
T E T O N   O R E   D O E
      M I N I S   R A D I U S
A S S   S I Z E S   E A T S
S T E A M B O A T W I L L I E
S I C S   D R E A M   S E N
E N R A P T   S T R O P
T E E   R A F   N A B E S
      T H E D U K E O F Y O R K
A D I O S   M A R D I   O N E
V I V R E   E N T E R   T I E
A G E N T   R E E S E   H E T
```

49

```
A B A T E   J I L T   T E A S
R A C E R   A N E W   O A T H
M Y C A R I S S O O L D T H E
F O R K   G O E S   A D E L A
U N E   D O N T   E I S N E R
L E T T E R   P A R   U T E
S T E A M   B Y E S   A P E D
      M I L E A G E I S
C A R P   O A K S   B E A S T
A D E   S G T   L E A N E R
P O T A T O   S P O T   I V E
T R I C E   A U R A   A M I S
I N R O M A N N U M E R A L S
V E E R   S T U D   B E L L E
E D E N   P E P E   B A S E S
```

50

```
O L D S   T B A R S   C H I P
D O R M   A R S O N   H E R O
I D E A   C O A T O F A R M S
N E S S   K I N   A S S A Y
      S H I L L   W A R E
S E C U R E   P A P E R B O Y
C R O P S   M I N E   S O S O
R I D   C A N E S   T S K
A C E S   E N O S   R E T I E
M A S T O D O N   T I L L E D
      A G E R   S H A L E
A P P L E   S H E   I C E D
B R A K E S H O E S   P A L O
L A V E   P U R E E   S P A T
E Y E R   Y E A R S   E S N E
```

51

```
K A M A   A R L E N   S P A M
A D A M   S H A D E   T O B E
S H R I N K I N G V I O L E T
E O N   A N N E E   S P O T S
M C E N R O E   H A I
O C T   B O O B T U B E
I R I S   H O R N E   L A V
W I T H E R I N G G L A N C E
A C E   G I D D Y   S A H L
S O M E O N E S   M A A
      M I D   S U R P A S S
A C H E S   A M I G A   R O I
S H O R T E N I N G B R E A D
P I N G   F O R G E   I N R E
S A K E   S N E E R   B A S S
```

52

```
T A R T S   J A M B   B U G S
A L A I N   A R I A   A L O T
P E P P E R M I N T P A T T Y
S E T T E E   U S O   I T E
      O R N A T E   M A M A S
A C M E S   W E T   P T A
L O A   P O L   B O O T I E
D A S H I E L L H A M M E T T
A T T I L A   O A R   L A T
      E E L   N F L   S T Y L E
H E R D S   O F L A T E
A R M   E S P   R U S T L E
D R I V E R E D U C A T I O N
T O N E   A T O P   R E D I D
O L D E   S S T S   T E E N S
```

53

```
A B B A   W O R K   C A B L E
S U E R   A R E A   A V O I D
S L A M   R E A P   L I O N S
      B R A H M S L U L L A B Y
M A T   S T O A T
D A L E T H S   S C E N D S
E T O N   K O R E A   O O P
B E D T I M E F O R B O N Z O
T U G   N A W A B   C E E S
S P E E C H   E L E C T R A
      R E D I D   A L A
S O M N I L O Q U I S T S
M A R I S   S A U R   I R A Q
I N A N E   A L A I   O U S T
O G L E D   S L Y E   N E E R
```

54

```
R A Y S   A M A Z E   P A W N
A L E C   C A R E Y   O C H O
I D L I K E T O S E E T H E M
D O P E Y   Z O T   P A Y E E
      N O L O   B O S
E J E C T A   T R A C H E A
C O M E O U T W I T H   L B J
O N O S   G R I S T   A I D A
L A T   C H I C K E N S O U P
H E L O I S E   R A T T L E
      E R N   T Y R E
U R B A N   A L I   C R E E P
F O R D U M M I E S S O U L S
O B I E   R E V U E   I R A S
S E E D   I N E P T   D O N T
```

55

```
A L L   C E L   S T A N
B O A T   F L O A T   L O G O
A G U A   O U N C E   Y U R T
S I G H T U N S E E N   C E E
E C H O I N G   M A S H E D
      E N D   G A S P E D
A D S   A R M O R   S C O P E
S E M I   Y O U N G   S W A N
S L E D S   A G O R A   N R A
L O C A T E   O U I
B A L L A D   S U N N I E R
A B A   T O O N E S T A S T E
L I R A   B R A V E   P L U G
E D A M   E A V E D   T A D A
S E T S   L E N   M E L
```

56

```
R E S E T   A L E R T   O R E
A B A B A   P I Q U E   V E X
C O V E R G R O U N D   E M U
E N E R G Y   N U S   G R I D
      T E R I   S U Z E T T E
A B C   T A R T   P A T H
H E A D S T A R T   G H E N T
A L P O   E Q U A L   O T O E
B L A N C   I M P O S T O R S
      N E O N   P E T E   P A T
F A D E O U T   D I C E
L A G S   C R O   O R D E R S
O R O   F L I P O N E S L I D
R O W   H E M A N   T E S L A
A N N   A I S L E   S L E E K
```

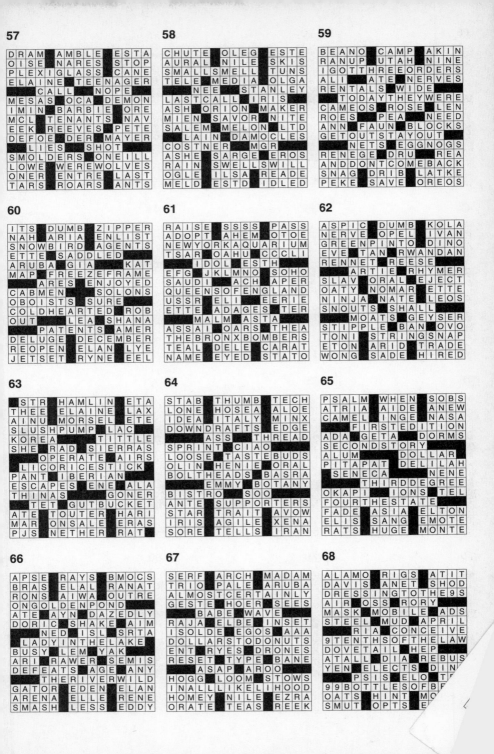

57

D R A M	A M B L E	E S T A
O I S E	N A R E S	S T O P
P L E X I G L A S S	C A N E
E L A I N E	T E E N A G E R
C A L L	N O P E
M E S A S	O C A	D E M O N
I M I N	B A R B I E	O R E
M C L	T E N A N T S	N A V
E E K	R E E V E S	P E T E
D E F O E	D E R	M A Y E R
L I E S	S H O T
S M O L D E R S	O N E I L L
L O W E	W E R E W O L V E S
O N E R	E N T R E	L A S T
T A R S	R O A R S	A N T S

58

CHUTE OLEG ESTE
AURAL NILE SKIS
SMALLSMELL TUNS
TELE MEDIA OLGA
NEE STANLEY
LASTCALL IRIS
ASH ORION MAKER
MIEN SAVOR NITE
SALEM MELON LTD
LAIN DAMOCLES
COSTNER MGR
ASHE SARGE EROS
RAIN SWELLSWILL
OGLE ILSA READE
MELD ESTD IDLED

59

BEANO CAMP AKIN
RANUP UTAH NINE
IGOTTHREEORDERS
ALI ATE NERVES
RENTALS WIDE
TODAYTHEYWERE
CAMEOS ROSE LEN
ROES PEA NEED
ANN FAUN BLOCKS
GETOUTSTAYOUT
NETS EGGNOGS
RENEGE DRU REA
ANDDONTCOMEBACK
SNAG DRIB LATKE
PEKE SAVE OREOS

60

ITS DUMB ZIPPER
NAH ARIA ENLIST
SNOWBIRD AGENTS
ETTE SADDLED
ARUBA GIA KAT
MAP FREEZEFRAME
ARES ENJOYED
CABMEN SOLONS
OBOISTS SURE
COLDHEARTED ROB
OUT LEA SHANA
DELUGE DECEMBER
REOPEN ELAN LYE
JETSET RYNE EEL

61

RAISE SSSS PASS
ADOPT AHEM OTOE
NEWYORKAQUARIUM
TSAR OAHU CCCLI
IDOL ESTH
EFG JKLMNO SOHO
SAUDI ACH APER
QUEENSOFENGLAND
USSR ELI EERIE
ETTE ADAGES TER
MALM ASTA
ASSAI OARS THEA
THEBRONXBOMBERS
TEAL DELE CARAT
NAME EYED STATO

62

ASPIC DUMB KOLA
NERVE OPEL IVAN
GREENPINTO DINO
EVE TAN RWANDAN
RENNET REESE
ARTIE RHYMER
SLAV ORAL EJECT
OATY NOMAR ETTE
NINJA NATE LEOS
SNOUTS SHALL
MOATS GEYSER
STIPPLE BAN OVO
TONI STRINGSNAP
ETON ARID TRADE
WONG SADE HIRED

63

STR HAMLIN ETA
THEE ELAINE LAX
AINU MORSEL ETE
SLUSHPUMP LAC
KOREA TITTLE
SHE RAD SIERRAS
OPERATE AIRS
LICORICESTICK
PANT IBERIAN
ESCAPES ENE ALA
THINAS GONER
TET GUTBUCKET
ATE TOUTER HARI
MAR ONSALE ERAS
PJS NETHER RAT

64

STAB THUMB TECH
LONE HOSEA ALOE
IDEA ITALY MINX
DOWNDRAFTS EDGE
ASS THREAD
SPRINT CIAO
LOOSE TASTEBUDS
OLIN HENIE ORAL
BOLTHEADS BASRA
EMMY BOTANY
BISTRO SOO
ANTE SUPPORTERS
STAR TRAIT AVOW
IRIS AGILE XENA
SORE TELLS IRAN

65

PSALM WHEN SOBS
ATRIA AIDE ANEW
CAMEL INGE NASA
FIRSTEDITION
ADA GETA DORMS
SECONDSTORY
ALUM DOLLAR
PITAPAT DELILAH
SENECA NENE
THIRDDEGREE
OKAPI IONS TEL
FOURTHESTATE
FADE ASIA ELTON
ELIS SANG EMOTE
RATS HUGE MONTE

66

APSE RAYS BMOCS
BRAS ELAL RANAT
RONS AIWA OUTRE
ONGOLDENPOND
ATE AYN DAZEDLY
DORIC SHAKE AIM
NED ISL SRTA
LADYINTHELAKE
BUSY LEM YAK
ARI RAWER SEMIS
DEFEATS AGE ANY
THERIVERWILD
GATOR EDEN ELAN
ARENA ELLE RENE
SMASH LESS EDDY

67

SERF ARCH MADAM
TRIO PALE ARUBA
ALMOSTCERTAINLY
GESTE HOER SEES
BABE WAVE
RAJA ELBE INSET
ISOLDE EGOS AAA
DOLLARSTODONUTS
ENT RYES DRONES
RESET TYPE BANE
ASAP AROO
HOGG LOOM STOWS
INALLLIKELIHOOD
HOMEY NILE EZRA
ORATE TEAS REEK

68

ALAMO RIGS ATIT
DAVIS ANET SHOD
DRESSINGTOTHE9S
AIR OSS RORY
MASK MOBILE ADS
STEEL MUD APRIL
RIA CONCEIVE
9TENTHSOFTHELAW
DOVETAIL HEP
ATALL DIA REBUS
YEN ELECTS DIN
PSIS ELO TE
99BOTTLESOFBE
OATS HINT MO
SMUT OPTS E

69

```
TAPS  AWASH  RASP
ONIT  TASTE  ALTO
PORE  TITAN  NCOS
LIONS  FRI  ADORE
INSOLE  INCLOVER
NTH  OLAN  POLED
EEK  POPGROUP
  DIP  OOO  HEM
  LANDFALL  TAM
STARR  PREY  HRE
INHUMANE  ALBERT
TARDY  EAT  EERIE
EREI  APRIL  REAR
MEAT  BALKY  MAGE
SSTS  ELSIE  SLED
```

70

```
PUSS  SLANG  CLIP
ANNA  COLON  HOME
STAMPOFAPPROVAL
SIR  ERASE  ERECT
ELEMENT  MBA
  YRS  STEALING
SPOT  SLANG  RAW
PUSHTHEENVELOPE
ACH  RAIDEN  ONAN
REAWAKEN  TKO
  ACE  SIAMESE
PROVE  BITTY  ATA
LOWERCASELETTER
OVER  BRAVE  HEAL
WEDS  SLANG  ENDS
```

71

```
MISDO  VISTA  MAT
OCHER  ALIEN  IRA
THEBLACKCAT  NAP
  ETON  SKIJUMP
ASP  NAIR  CUTIE
CHIC  SMOCK  JEST
SUSHI  BUREAU
  THEWHITEALBUM
  COMBED  TEPID
SOAK  SERIF  SHEA
UNCUT  STOP  END
NITPICK  RATA
LOO  THEREDROVER
INN  LEROY  TRAWL
TSE  ERNIE  SELES
```

72

```
BARED  AWES  RATS
ADELE  SALE  OLIO
BUNKERHILL  UPTO
ALT  DUES  LAGOON
STATEN  TEETH
  REAL  PRORATA
ASEA  TATI  NINES
TAMPS  TAC  EDNAS
ODIST  ERAS  EAST
PERHAPS  LAHR
  ORATE  DESPOT
TAROTS  RIAL  ANE
HOOT  SUITTOATEE
ANTE  ONCE  TURIN
NEER  SIAM  SKINS
```

73

```
CAPP  ONEARM  QED
OPER  DARNAY  UMA
APRONSTRING  IMF
CLIVE  STOODPAT
HES  EMI  RUSE
  HANGBYATHREAD
  SABLE  NERO
MARSH  ECT  PIKES
IDEA  CHORE
  DOWNTOTHEWIRE
  TYNE  YES  UPS
PREERECT  MANIC
RAD  ACHORUSLINE
EGG  NANTES  ICON
ZEE  TROOPS  TENT
```

74

```
GIZA  SLAP  BAJA
ROIL  SHIRR  ALAS
OTTO  PATIO  BUNK
WAITERWHATCOMES
  GAL  OHO
SALARY  LAZINESS
ERASE  KILO  MTA
WITHTHEMEATLOAF
ESE  APEX  OUTRE
DENTISTS  ANGERS
  ANT  CST
ASINCEREAPOLOGY
HANK  NOLTE  OPIE
ONCE  ELLEN  LAVA
YEAR  DEAR  ALES
```

75

```
HALF  CHAFF  CBS
AVIAN  NACRE  HAL
HEAVEANCHOR  USA
ARROWS  KENTUCKY
  REPO  DIRKS
PEP  RIBS  SLAW
ASIS  COLT  ENACT
LATH  EER  UGLY
LUCIE  SEED  SOUR
  HERB  PARR  NEE
  ABLER  TOAD
WILDCATS  ODESSA
AMA  THROWPILLOW
DEC  EMILE  OHARA
IRK  DAMES  ITTY
```

76

```
CAVS  MOANS  EKES
ARIA  EDSEL  LEVY
SINKONESMONEYIN
AZTECS  OPENED
BON  TACT  LADEN
ANEW  HAVES  INA
SARA  CAMARO  NTH
  DROPALINE
GAB  ADELIE  DUCT
ANA  MALES  ONOR
LIBRA  SERA  TRI
MYOPIC  INMATE
FALLONHARDTIMES
OTOE  KATIE  LEGO
PENS  STEPS  EDEN
```

77

```
NESS  DABS  SHOT
OCTO  ERST  EMERY
SHELLGAME  AONES
HOTAIR  TIPTOP
  SEA  GASCAPS
REGALERS  RAHRAH
ELOPE  LEGIT  TRI
DALE  MEALS  DIEN
DID  PASTO  BRENT
ONEPER  SANJUSTO
GENETIC  TIO
  ELROYS  ERECTS
BUGLE  CHICKPEAS
ANGEL  LONE  EDIT
HOST  EEKS  EELS
```

78

```
  THAT  ZEST  GRAB
ERATO  APSE  LONE
TALON  NINA  ESTA
HISPANIC  MYNAHS
ANT  LEE  UNLIT
NEON  ESTEEM  ILL
SENTA  RELY  ELY
  HERBARIUM
SOB  RAID  MARSH
EMO  INDEED  TOTO
RIATA  TRA  ARR
ITSELF  THYMUSES
ATTA  LARA  ANTAE
TEER  ETON  ITEMS
DDY  WADE  NODS
```

79

```
SHIRT  PSAT  YULE
NATES  ACME  ANOX
ABASE  PHON  WHIP
FILO  SPARTA  OTO
UTILITYVEHICLES
SCENE  MOIRE
  CRANIA  LEE
INTHEVANGUARD
NOR  SEVERE
ASSAY  ELOPE
JEEPERSCREEPERS
OCC  SEALED  ETAL
BUOY  AMEN  ANISE
ORNE  CORE  METED
NEER  HAKE  PRESS
```

80

```
WASP  ANDI  FLY
ESTES  MIAMI  LIE
SHARPWITTED  AMA
TENURE  ELECTOR
  SEAT  DAHS
SNEERER  ALLIED
SNO  EXEC  SOLVE
PITA  RATED  EVAN
UPEND  SISI  EDS
REWORD  ETAGERE
  ODIE  ABRA
CAREENS  LUGGED
OTT  STAFFOFLIFE
OOH  TAKER  FELTS
SPY  LIDO  TASK
```

81

```
I N F O . A P S E S . M U T E
L E A P . B R E T T . O P R Y
L A Z E . J A P E R . H O U R
. T E N C E N T S A D A N C E .
. . B A C K . P O I . .
T A P O U T . S U P E R M A N
O L I O S . B A S E . A N I
N I C K E L A N D D I M I N G
G M T . A S T A . D I N A H
A B S I N T H E . W I S E S T
. . N A H . R I O T . .
Q U A R T E R M A S T E R S .
U N D O . R A L P H . R O A M
I T Z A . E L L I E . E L K O
T O E D . D E E D S . D Y E D
```

82

```
L A S H . S P A D E . H A L S
E L L A . C A R E T . A B E T
G O O D T I M E C H A R L I E
S T E E R . . A C I D T E S T
. . S E A M . A C E . .
B O S . B L A M . S N A P U P
A V A . L A M A R . N E H I
B E T T E R M O U S E T R A P
E R I E . A R B O R . S U E
S T E N C H . I L S A . E L S
. . L O S . E A S E . .
A N I S E T T E . E D D I E
B E S T F O O T F O R W A R D
B O L O . I N T E R . I N O N
A N E W . L E A N S . N A N A
```

83

```
S H E S . S T E R . J A D E D
M I S T . C I T E . O H A R E
A P S E . R E A D . Y O D E L
S P E N C E R T R A C Y . .
H O N O R E E . O N E . A S A
. . . E N D I V E . J U T S
S P L I T . R E A . A T O P
L I O N E L B A R R Y M O R E
A K I N . E A T . E B S E N
P E N S . G R E A T S . . .
S R S . R A F . S H E A V E S
. . W A L L A C E S H A W N
L O G I C . I C E S . E L E E
I N U S E . E N N E . A U R A
D A T E D . S E T S . D E S K
```

84

```
. R I C O . M A R T . S H E
. D E C O R . A S E A . C O S
T O G E T B A C K O N . A M P
A R E A S . T H E . S O R E R
L I N G . S H O W . G I B E
C A T E R T O . I D L E R S
. I R M A . R E E S E S .
Y O U R F E E T M I S S T W O
A N N A L S . M A S K . . .
M E S H E S . R E S O L E D
M O M A . C A T S . R E D O
E N O L A . A S H . A W A I T
R O K . C A R P A Y M E N T S
E N E . D O L E . M O L T S
R E D . C L A N . A R L O
```

85

```
M E D I C . H A T . D E F T
I R A T E . A L E C . I V E S
C O S T A . T I N A . L A V A
A S H . S P E E D R E A D E R
. B L E E D . . E A T E R
C L O U D S . S T E V E . .
R O A R . O C T A N E . R A W
O G R E S . O A R . D O U G H
W E D . C A R G O S . K N E E
. . B A L K S . A P I A R Y
L A U R A . . E A S E R .
H U R R Y S C U R R Y . O A T
A N O N . K O N G . C H U T E
N A M E . A L T O . H O N E R
G R A D . T O T . O G D E N
```

86

```
R A S H . M A L T . B A T H E
A S T A . I S A Y . I L I A D
D I O R . S H I P . K E M P T
A D V A N C E N O T I C E .
R E E S E . . S A N . S T D
. . S W A M P . R I C H E R
A F B . E L I O T . E A S E
P R O G R E S S R E P O R T S
T A X I . S T E A L . E S S
E M O T E D . S E R U M . .
R E F . G E M . T E N T S
. F O R W A R D M O T I O N
A L I V E . R A R E . H E R E
R I C E S . S T A T . O C T A
T E E N S . H E W S . D E S K
```

87

```
M I D I . M A A M . T A I G A
E R R S . U R N E . H I R A M
O M A R . S A I D . E M I L E
W A B A S H B L U E S . S A N
. . E A R . S L A B . .
. Y E L L O W H A M M E R S
S U R . T O Y A . E T H A N
S K A T . M O D E M . S O M E
N O T R E . A R A T . D O W
. N O I S E T T E R O S E S .
. . P T E R . I N A . .
O P S . O R A N G E S M A S H
R O W A N . C O L T . P L E A
S W A M I . E R A T . L U N T
O S T I A . D A D A . E M T S
```

88

```
P I E S . C A S S . T Y R O L
A N A T . O N E A . R I A T A
S T R A W P O L L . A E G I S
S O N N Y T U F T S . L E S T
. D E S K . . E N D . .
V A D I S . S A R A . M G T
A B E S . D E A L I N . O R A
D A P H N E D U M A U R I E R
E T O . A T O N A L . A R E S
R E T . R A M A . O M A N I
. . C C C . R A S P . .
S O P H . H E L E N H A Y E S
U R I A H . T E E N A G E R S
M E T R O . A N K A . E T A T
S L A T E . L A S S . S I T S
```

89

```
R A M P . S T A I R . B A T S
O M A R . P A N D A . U N I T
T A X I . A S T E R . D E M O
T I M O N T I M E A G A I N
. . U K E . . N E R D Y
S A L A R Y . C R U S T . .
E M I T . . S A O N E . B A A
R O M E O A N D J U L I E T C
A S P . P R A D O . S T A R
. . S E E P Y . P A R A D E
A R O A R . . N O R . .
R I C H A R D I I I T I M E
U V E A . A U N T S . S O R T
B E A R . M E T R E . T R I O
A N N A . S T O O D . O N C E
```

90

```
M A L T . T W A S . C O S M O
O B O E . E A R P . H I T O N
T O O T . N I L E . A L I V E
H U S H E D T O N E S . L E S
S T E E D S . . T O T A L .
. . R I T E S . N E L L I E
I L K . T O W E L S . A I D A
S E E P S . E W E . I N F E R
L O P E . T R U N K S . E S S
E N T R E E . P A I L S . .
. Q U I R E . . T A C O M A
L O U . S I L E N T M O V I E
A S I A N . I S E E . R E D S
T H E R E . A T T N . E R G O
E A T E R . S A S S . S T E P
```

91

```
R I G U P . P E I . S T A B S
O R A T E . O L D . H O S E A
W I R E R . S E A . A P T E R
E S A . K I T C H E N S I N K
R E G R E T . T O N G A . .
. . E N D E R . C H I D E S
P A B A . M O M S . A L E R T
A B A . T S U N A M I . N I A
W I N C E . T O R I . A M E S
S E D A N S . I N T R O . .
. . S C O O T . I R I T I S
C L O S E T D R A M A . H M O
H O P I N . D O W . I D E A L
A V A N T . E V E . N O R G E
D E L I S . R E D . S A S E S
```

92

```
S C A M . B U R M A . A R B S
E L S E . A N E A R . S E E P
W I T T . R I B T I C K L E R
. M R S . . U T A H . A L I
O B I . . S A F E . A S T I N
K I D S T U F F . . K E N T
S N E E R E R . P O M A D E S
. . D I D O . E M I T . .
S T J A M E S . D E L E T E D
N A U T . R A G T R A D E
O D D E R . B E L A . L A P
W P A . A M A S . . A L S
J O S H M O S T E L . R Y
O L E O . S T U N G . C
B E S T . T E P E E . H
```

93

```
STRIP  ELECT  SAW
SAUNA  BUGLE  EKE
EDGARBERGEN   NIL
     TIRE   VAPORS
ADJUNCT   DEBORAH
CRISES   CURLEW
ELMER  HALLE  EPA
RAMS   FOLLY  SNUB
BOY  SLAVS  NACRE
   NATURE  MOLEST
FUELROD   GENESES
OILIER   ARTS
RNS  WILLIETYLER
ATO  EDITS  OOOLA
YAN  DEPOT  PUNKY
```

94

```
FRA  GOTIT  SHARE
LIT  EVADE  HOGAN
ACT  SARAS  ACRID
WHISTLESTOP   ADE
EERIE   EWE   REA
DRED  SHADE  BIRR
    ITER   BRASS
  CONURBATION
CAINE   ODIN
OPTS  PARSE  STAY
UPI   EON   SLAVE
RAF  MEGALOPOLIS
ARISE  EMILE  LAS
GEESE  LARGE  ETE
ELDER  STEAD  RED
```

95

```
ACHES  EBAN  BARB
RHONE  QUAY  OGEE
CARVEOUTACAREER
STAYSPUT   TENSE
      TAS  QUARTET
RETOOL   FUND
ATARI  SLIT  IDLE
PAINTTHETOWNRED
STLO  HOES  IRANI
   GEES   SPIGOT
CASHIER   LIE
ETHAN   SOLOISTS
DRAWACONCLUSION
EIRE  HOOK  TITLE
SAID  APBS  STELE
```

96

```
EMILE  SWIG  RITA
TOLER  LANA  HOST
HOOTENANNY   ETAT
ERN  CAPE  NOTARY
REACTS   SNORT
   ASAP   ARABIAN
SIMP  LONG  LUSTY
AGATE  TOG  STERE
NORAD  TREY  LEAS
ARTISTE   DOGE
   NERDS   KARRAS
MUSCLE  POUR  ABA
OLEO  MAIDMARIAN
ONTO  OGRE  NOLTE
TASK  REOS  DOSER
```

97

```
SKIN  DRAG  SHAME
TITO  OAHU  HARES
OKLAHOMASOONERS
WILHELM   BONNIE
    RIENZI   ATTN
OKTOBERFEST
TARP  CAPO  PSI
ATATURK   LOGSOUT
YEP  NAIL   ELLA
  OKSANABAIUL
STAR   ESTATE
TAHITI   PRESSES
OKEFENOKEESWAMP
NEALE  FORS  ABIE
ENDED  FOYT  MUTE
```

98

```
JAMES  ONLY  CALF
IMUST  LEIA  APER
VISTA  LETTERSTO
EEC  LAID  ATEAM
   OPINE   OGRE
  OVINE  SVETLANA
STIES  TOOTH  LAX
TATS  CARLA  ALTI
ARE  PLUTO  ALIAS
RUSSIANS   OFALL
    TENT   PERDU
UNIAT  IASI  YOM
SOCIALIST   ENERO
EWER  IDLE  NEVER
RIDS  BOER  DEALT
```

99

```
IPSO  COLT   HATE
COOP  ODEA  LETIN
COMEAPART   ELENA
  HENNYYOUNGMAN
  TED  IMISSMY
EVIDENT   SLIM
DIM  SERA   TAFFY
DEER  WIFES  NOLA
ATSEA  TRAM  OUR
   TSPS  SLOTTED
COOKING   TAR
  ASOFTENASICAN
OVOLO  LOCOFOCOS
FILER  LMNO  MEAL
FLED   SEEN  ASHY
```

100

```
GUAM  RAPT    ASA
AFRO  ADIOS  BLOC
MOTORMOUTH   UTAH
ESS  EBBS  ELMORE
   TALE   FLIP
JANICE   CULDESAC
OPART  TINE  ROBE
LADE  TODDY  CLOD
TREE  OWES  CRAVE
STRAINER   SHORES
   SOIL  SHIP
SKIING  COAL  OVA
WILL  HOODWINKED
ALLY  TIDAL  ARIZ
POS   LESS  GALE
```